Gardening Nature's Way

Gardening Nature's Way

The Secrets of Creating an Organic Garden

THELMA BARLOW

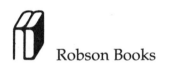

Robson Books

This edition first published in Great Britain in 2000 by
Robson Books, 10 Blenheim Court,
Brewery Road, London N7 9NT

A member of the Chrysalis Group plc

First published by Robson Books in 1992 as
Organic Gardening with Love

British Library Cataloguing in Publication Data
A catalogue record for this book is available from the
British Library

ISBN 0 86105 331 2

Typeset by Columns Design Limited, Reading
Printed in Great Britain by Butler & Tanner Ltd, Frome and London

Contents

For those who are and those who will become organic gardeners.

Acknowledgements

There are people to thank for their stoic stifling of yawns as I chattered on long after their interest in my project had waned. People to thank for their encouragement and help, people who share a love of gardening, a sense of proportion and a sense of humour. All are dear well-loved friends, some are mentioned in the book, some are not, but all of them are an important part of my life.

I must particularly thank Clive Dickinson for his patience in listening to my ramblings and structuring them so expertly, my sister Veda, my friend of many years, David Trevena, and Jo Taylor, my gardener, for reading and advising on the manuscript. Thanks too to David Thompson for his splendid line drawings.

Lastly, and no small task in their busy lives, I thank Alan and Jackie Gear of the Henry Doubleday Research Association for reading the whole book, cover to cover, to save me the embarrassment of having misguided any potential reader.

Most sincere and grateful thanks to all.

Foreword

Given the current threats to the environment – including the destruction of tropical rain forests, pollution of the oceans and global warming – it's not surprising that many people feel helpless. What can a mere individual do to change things for the better?

Well, in your garden at least, by gardening organically, you can do your bit for planet Earth. If you stop using pesticides wildlife won't be poisoned and by not buying artificial fertilizers you are less likely to pollute underground water supplies.

Thelma Barlow, in her idyllic plot in the Pennines, gardens organically and this book is all about why and how she does it. In essence she works with, rather than against, nature – using compost and natural manures to build up a healthy soil, so as to provide plants with a diet that gives them natural resistance to pests and diseases.

Like all of us, Thelma has her gardening successes and failures. How nice it would be, for instance, to be able to grow hostas without having to worry about slugs! Still, I suppose, if we knew all the answers, it would take the fun out of gardening.

I was delighted when Thelma asked me to write this Foreword, for I know her to be a keen and knowledgeable gardener. I couldn't recommend this book more strongly whether you're planning to take up gardening for the first time, or if you're thinking about switching to organic methods. Her compassion and humility are an inspiration to gardeners everywhere. Once I picked up the book I read it from cover to cover. I'm sure you'll do the same.

Alan Gear
Chief Executive
The Henry Doubleday Research Association

Introduction

Anxieties about conservation and environmental pollution were only faintly-heard rumblings about nineteen years ago, when I chose to become an organic gardener. I was fortunate at that time to read a brief mention in a magazine about an organic gardening movement in Essex and on receipt of more information I promptly joined the HDRA as a life member. It all made such good sense and promised, what is more, to be ethically very satisfying.

Since then I have become totally devoted to this way of gardening which is, in fact, a return to the natural methods of the past made more sophisticated and effective by the addition of up-to-date research and scientifically safe and proved techniques.

There has been, and still is, much to learn. There have been, and always will be, mistakes to be made – triumphs and failures. There were temptations at first; as a plague of aphids descended on the garden, my hand would hover over the chemical insecticide which I knew would zap them into oblivion – but I just couldn't do it. Shakespeare wrote: 'Conscience doth make cowards of us all' – well, there have to be exceptions to the Bard's truisms, and my conscience was now so well and truly aware of the damage I would be doing to the balance of wildlife in my garden that I decided to be a brave and true organic gardener, harness the many cunning and devious methods of natural pest control, show a little patience and understanding and put my trust in the voracious appetites of the predators I hoped I had attracted to my little plot in the North Yorkshire Dales.

It worked. I can never be less than overwhelmed by the vitality and life force of nature at work in my garden. The clay soil I inherited was dull and fairly lifeless, untamed, stony beyond belief, heavily compacted once the turf was removed and sporting a few anaemic-looking worms and little else – not very promising. Nineteen years later, after constant additions of composts and mulches of one kind and another, it is teeming with life, much easier to work (although stones still proliferate) and supports a veritable jungle of decorative and edible shrubs, trees and wildlife in great variety. Even the once-anaemic worms have come on a treat and by their presence and activity I know that my soil is in good heart.

When I was first asked to write this book I thought long and hard – after all, what I do is act – I'm hardly qualified to be giving advice on organic gardening. In fact though, the two subjects do have a deal in common: both are creative, both involve giving and taking and both can be demanding and at the same time therapeutic.

My many years working in television has brought me close to millions of viewers – we have formed a bond. I think perhaps through this book I might reach many who are also gardeners and perhaps they will be fired by my enthusiasm for organic gardening, throw out all their expensive sprays and paraphernalia and join the ever-increasing band of people who are trying to nurture a good healthy environment in their own God-given plot.

I hope you will be inspired to try *Gardening Nature's Way*.

Thelma Barlow

1 Finding My Way to Organic Gardening

'A green thought in a green shade.'

Andrew Marvell
'The Garden'

Gardening for me hasn't been without its shades and not all of them where I would have wished, but I'll come to those later. It's the green thoughts that have brought me lasting pleasure for as long as I remember – literally. Three years of my very young life were spent in the country and I think I have more vivid memories of that time than any other.

Working in the theatre isn't always the most settled existence! Mine has had me living in London, the West of England, Birmingham, Nottingham, Bristol, Glasgow, Altrincham and Manchester, but my heart and home have always been in Yorkshire. That's where I was born and that's where I've lived in my cottage and garden in the Dales for the last nineteen years.

Middlesbrough was the setting for my earliest memories. I returned there some years ago to open a children's painting exhibition and the mayor took me in his limousine back to Falmouth Street, where I was born. It's like a little Coronation Street. Some of the houses have smarter doors and windows than I would have known. But otherwise it hasn't changed from the familiar pattern of a window and a door, a window and a door, a window and a door, with a couple of steps leading up to each house. I couldn't remember our number accurately, but we had our photograph taken outside one of the houses, the mayor and I.

There was hardly any garden in Falmouth Street to sow the early seeds of my love of natural things, though uncles and aunts had gardens which may have kindled my interest. (Unlikely though it seems, I've come to the conclusion that my many other memories from before I was three pointed to the fact that I would become an actress.)

My father died just six weeks before I was born which must have been a terrible tragedy for the household: my mother, my sister, my grandmother and me. His death left us very hard up. At the time I was born there was twenty-seven and sixpence coming into the house each week: my mother's widow's pension of ten shillings, another ten shillings for my grandmother in her old age, five shillings for my older sister and half-a-crown for me.

Living on what in today's money would be £1.37½ made it very difficult to struggle along, as I obviously realized even from the depths of my cot. I still have a clear memory of Mum stopping behind me, when we were out one day with the pushchair. The hood was up and I could hear her talking to another lady. There was the sound of sympathetic voices (not that I knew they were sympathetic, but I must have picked something up from the tone of what they were saying). Eventually the lady put her head around the hood and I knew that I was expected to respond to these sounds and the expression on her face. I had to appear pathetic. So I looked up sorrowfully and sadly and won an appropriate response from my 'audience'.

I think Mum worried that I was rather a weak child and moving to the country to live next door to my grandmother's sister when I was three seemed like a good idea. I couldn't have agreed with her more.

Our new home in Hutton Rudby made such an impact on me that my childhood memories from those years are filled with images of playing in the woods and fields, gathering flowers, mushrooms and brambles, and enjoying all the simple pleasures of a country childhood.

I like to think I had an innate feeling for the countryside. My love of nature, wildlife and all growing things blossomed in the three years that we lived in our little whitewashed cottage, clustered along with three others in that tiny village below the Cleveland Hills. A lot of people living there now commute to Middlesbrough every day which would have been unthinkable when I was a little girl living what seemed miles from anywhere.

We had a small garden with nice old lavenders, southernwood (which we called by its country name Lad's Love), and roses growing over the doorways. 'Playing-out' was marvellous with all the space of the fields and gardens to enjoy. We used to love picking lots of wild flowers and taking them to a telegraph pole in jam jars pretending it was a grave; playing funerals was a favourite game!

Village pastimes were simple and 'homemade' too. At Easter everyone would paint Pace Eggs. (We had an egg-rolling ceremony down the hills as well.) Gathering flowers and leaves and wrapping them round the eggs before we boiled them, so that the dye would come out to decorate the shell, was a yearly ritual which we always looked forward to, and a tradition I still keep.

One of Mum's friends, Mrs Wilson, had a small-holding where we used to go, in spite of unwelcome attention at times from the hens and geese. (My sister blames her fear of birds on Mrs Wilson's fowls and I had my own mixed feelings about the geese which supplied the goose grease which was rubbed on my chest whenever I showed signs of being poorly.) Her fields led down to a wood with a little beck which was a favourite place for 'primrosing'. As the youngest I was always too small to leap across the stream and invariably missed the bank and fell into the water, for which I knew I could expect a good scolding. Little hands wringing out cotton socks were pretty ineffective and squelchy leather sandals didn't always escape Grandma's beady eye when they returned home.

Taking the edge off this country idyll were mundane necessities like the outside earth closet where beady eyes were once more likely to be encountered – but this time accompanied by clucking and flying feathers as the neighbours' hens were evicted for the sake of privacy. It wasn't just the loo that was outside then, we had to go out to the pump with a bucket whenever we wanted water; and the milkman used to bring us milk in a little pony and trap – in churns. We'd go out to the gate with a jug for him to ladle out however much we wanted. He would also take his customers to the station, not that many people from the village normally went to the station. A muffin man used to call as well, carrying the muffins and pikelets in a huge basket covered with a snowy white cloth.

To lessen the number of trips to the pump, our hair was washed in the rainwater collected in the butt beside the house. Tiny little pink worms lived in it and I was terrified that they might take up residence in my head; if my friends read this they might think it explains a lot!

I was six when we moved to West Yorkshire. Mum had become quite a regular helper in the vicarage at Hutton Rudby and when the vicar became a canon in Huddersfield she was persuaded to help his family settle into their new house in Edgerton. After a few months a small house close to theirs became available and Mum's temporary arrangement became more or less permanent, which meant the excitement of a removal van at the door of our cottage and the longest journey of my life, across Yorkshire in a bus to our new home.

Even though we were just a mile from the centre of Huddersfield, there were still open fields to enjoy. They were, we discovered, just across the road from us. (They still are as it happens, and so is the old bus shelter.) I don't know why that land has remained undeveloped but it was home from home for us as children. Here was another little beck to play in. We used to dig for hairy nuts, which we washed in the water and then gobbled up. I'm sure they must be a sort of poor man's truffle, as their other name is 'pig nut'. We thought they tasted delicious. Sadly, if you eat them, the plant's gone, of course, but environmental considerations like that still hadn't fully dawned on me at that age.

Not that they were far away. Nature studies at school saw to this. We used to have a big wall chart listing all the flowers we were likely to come across and every spring there was great competition among us to see who could be the first to spot each celandine, or coltsfoot, snowdrop, harebell or whichever it was. The successful child had his or her name written on the chart alongside the flower, giving the date and place of its discovery. Year by year the charts built up a very interesting picture of where and when each season arrived and nature's year of new life began. They also kept us very observant and I suppose they helped me develop a way of seeing things in detail that's stood me in good stead on stage and screen, as well as in searching out greenfly or battling with slugs at home in the garden.

My senior school had once been a large private house surrounded by lovely grounds. We approached it down a beautiful drive full of rhododendrons and lined with beeches. But it was wartime when I arrived. This somehow had its impact on our hockey pitch which seemed to be waterlogged for the duration, depriving us of traditional winter games. We didn't fare much better in summer since the tennis courts had been converted into a 'victory garden' in which, class by class, we trenched in celery or dug up potatoes, to do our bit on the home front. It can't have been the most inspiring introduction to gardening. Though it can't have had any detrimental effect on me. I was already hooked.

My aunts and uncles up in the North-East gardened meticulously and I was always interested to go out with them and pick the gooseberries, water the plants and generally help as best I could.

And that more or less set the pattern of my gardening for a good many years to come.

From school I went straight to work in an office, a bread-winner at last, to the unspoken relief of Mum, I'm sure, who'd been coping tirelessly on her own until my sister and I were old enough to start earning our keep.

For my part the future seemed pointed unerringly towards the world of commerce. My final terms at school had been spent acquiring shorthand and typing skills (for which I was later to be immensely grateful) and I signed up with a friend for a further two years of night school following that. After the first year, however, my enthusiasm had started to wane slightly and when my friend agreed that another twelve months would be too much to bear, we looked around for something else to do. She was keen on music. I wasn't, particularly. The one thing we could agree on to do together was speech training and drama, and it didn't take me long after starting that to realize that the stage was beckoning far more enticingly than the office.

Like so many actors who've been fortunate in their careers, I was blessed with great good luck. Private training and a lot of work with good amateur groups in Huddersfield gave me a start. Then a young man, Kenneth Mellor, who designed sets (and as it happens has also designed my new conservatory) suggested that I should audition at the Civic Theatre, Bradford. At that time Bradford had a very good theatre school and many of its pupils who went on to the London stage used to come home when they weren't working there to direct and act at the Civic. For those of us in the company this seemed like a heaven-sent opportunity to work with up-and-coming professionals.

I was every bit as lucky in having an understanding boss in the daytime, who gave me time off from my 'real' secretarial job to do some broadcasting with the BBC and fit in other stage commitments as they cropped up.

Five years of work on the amateur stage in

Bradford and Huddersfield convinced me that I too should turn professional and try my luck in London. Mum was appalled at the idea and I think I only got away thanks to my shorthand and typing, which she reckoned would keep me out of harm's way if the stage couldn't.

Luckily for me, and perhaps any would-be employer, I didn't have to fall back on secretarial work for long. Within a year London led to a professional job in the West of England and, as it turned out, marriage as well. Work with the Liverpool Playhouse company followed; next came Birmingham Repertory and then Nottingham Playhouse. After work in the West End my husband and I were on the move again, this time to Bristol to join the Old Vic company at the Theatre Royal.

Apart from tending the small garden that came with our Birmingham flat, my work in those years spared very little time for gardening, especially as during our sojourn in Nottingham our first son, Clive, had been born.

The move to Bristol brought with it another piece of amazingly good luck. We rented a flat in a house owned by a keen gardener, far more knowledgeable than I could ever hope to be. We formed a lasting friendship and we now go on a gardening holiday together every year. This friend, Joan Keeling, and I managed to produce our second children within thirty-six hours of each other in the same house! So we had more than gardening in common.

Joan was the first person who inspired me to become interested in gardening in a more serious way. With her I learned to look at plants more closely. Her garden had a lot of old roses and with her encouragement and enthusiasm I started to appreciate their beauty and subtlety as individual plants and flowers, instead of as just part of a lovely garden.

We settled in Bristol and started buying our own house, which had a small garden front and back. This is where I had my first introduction to slugs, creatures with whom I've had an uneasy relationship ever since. The repulsion I experienced at finding a four-inch shiny black slug crawling over my shoe and on to my ankle has lasted as a very unsavoury memory to this day.

Working at the Bristol Old Vic then was exciting and rewarding, which was just as well since I found myself being the breadwinner while my husband was taking a degree at the university. During this time I was helped by three lovely au pairs who were each with us for a year, while I yo-yoed between home and theatre. One of the virtues of being born under the sign of Gemini (even on the cusp) is that I cheerfully agree to take on far too much, and then somehow muddle through – and this was a period of my life when muddling through was somehow the order of the day.

After getting Clive and James off to school I'd catch the bus to the theatre in the centre of town for ten o'clock rehearsals. After rehearsing all day I'd catch the bus back home to Redland at five-thirty, spend some time with the children at tea, in the bath or reading bedtime stories, then back to the theatre for 'the half', our call at five to seven for the evening show. Another bus-ride had me home by half-past ten or eleven to learn lines before going to sleep – all this, and matinees twice a week.

In between we lived a normal family life! I even

did a little gardening and there was always Joan in Cotham to keep me up to scratch, though I knew I'd never master the Latin names of my plants with anything like the dedication that she had. I've settled for a relaxed (lazier) approach which seems to keep me and my plants perfectly happy.

After eight years in Bristol, work took us to Glasgow; this move was not a successful one for my personal life, and the little gardening I did there reflected this. Eventually good luck smiled upon me once more and Granada offered me a long contract in *Coronation Street*, which meant a move south to be near the studios. I chose a house in Altrincham and started gardening in earnest.

This was to be my Garden of Eden. Altrincham has always been an excellent area for market gardening – the soil is wonderful, like black pastry crumbs. However, like Eden, my garden had not suffered unduly from the work of man. In fact it was a wreck and it took a lot of work of woman to bring it under something like control.

I faced privet standing about twenty feet high, ragged and straggly at the bottom with convolvulus growing right through the top of it. Then there was the huge purple beech which was lovely but shaded about a third of the garden.

The wretched convolvulus came through from the neighbour's garden, I discovered. They didn't do a thing about it, so I was faced with sieving the soil in an entire border to be sure of removing every trace of it; leaving only a bit of it behind would have had it sprouting vigorously back into life again. All that work! Had I known more about companion planting, I might have had the answer at my fingertips.

Slowly what seemed like a never-ending

struggle became easier. The garden started to look happier, more as I wanted it to look. I built a little rockery, a pergola, put up fencing for climbing plants, started a herbaceous border and a herb garden. With care and affection it ceased to look neglected and within the six years I lived there had become an absorbing hobby. I suppose what I'd originally started as a sort of relaxation therapy became more and more fun. I enjoyed experimenting with things and somewhere along the line I read about growing herbs and all their various uses. Without really realizing it, I was taking my first willing steps towards organic gardening.

This struck an immediate chord and I went right out and bought what I still think is the best book about herbs, Donald Law's *Herbal Encyclopaedia*. I find this so nicely put together that reading about the plants takes you effortlessly into all sorts of other subjects. It led to my discovering the properties of natural healing, homoeopathic medicines and flower remedies, all of which I've found to be completely in tune with my thinking about medical treatment, and highly beneficial to my health and well-being. This led naturally to an interest and concern about diet, the origin of the food we eat and the water we drink, which in turn led on to the wider question of the environmental problems here at home, and, wider than that, the global problems of pollution and commercial greed.

So, from thinking it might be nice to have bushes of rosemary, sage and thyme at the door for handy additions to the teapot or casserole, I became totally beguiled by the many paths which beckoned. An interest in plants can lead in so many different directions – through myth and legend, natural history, art, topography, literature, medicine, crafts, cooking. There's an endless array of intriguing possibilities; there's never a hope of learning enough, but never a chance to feel bored or complacent. I take comfort in the words of none other than Socrates who was once moved to remark, 'The more I know, the more I know how little I know.'

❂   HERBS FOR HEALING

My Altrincham soil was already providing me with parsley the like of which I have never seen before or since. Now I was led into planting and collecting the herbs, making herbal medicines, cooking with them and making wine.

In the end a good third of the garden was given over to herbs, dotted about between paving stones in a sort of random clock pattern. Thirty or forty different herbs kept me busy – and they all grew wonderfully.

There are lots of good herbal books around now and many excellent qualified herbalists, but to give an idea of the restorative properties waiting to be discovered (and enjoyed) here is a selection of herbal infusions that have either been tried by me and found to be effective, or have been recommended by friends. I must stress, however, the need to obtain qualified assistance for anything other than minor ailments.

As a general rule one of the commonest ways of making herbal remedies and herbal teas is to pour 1 pint of boiling water on to $1/2$–1 ounce of dried herbs in a ceramic jug or teapot. Let the brew stand for 10–15 minutes before straining and using the tea, adding honey if it's preferred by whoever's drinking it.

Now for the ailments, which I've put in alphabetical order because they range from arthritis to warts, just to show how many of life's aches, pains and general discomforts can be treated by one's own produce.

❁ *Arthritis and rheumatism*

Try nettle tea or sage tea, or the two mixed together. Prepare either or both of them by mixing 1 ounce of nettles and/or sage to 1 pint of water.

Chewing raw garlic eases discomfort too – persuade your nearest and dearest to join in!

Drinking a glass of celery tea a day also brings relief. Boil a few stalks, or half a head in 1 pint of water for half an hour.

You might like to try adding celery leaves or primrose leaves to salad.

Honeysuckle flowers, prepared as a tea using 4 or 5 flowers to 1 pint of water, have been easing aching joints for centuries. Drink one wineglassful every three hours.

❁ *Bronchitis and colds, catarrh and laryngitis*

Blackcurrant tea made with fresh berries is wonderful. A lot of proprietary remedies you find in chemists' shops use blackcurrant of course, but check that *real* blackcurrant is used.

Garlic, eaten raw is a great help, if you can bear it.

Coltsfoot tea is also good when you've got a

cold. Mix about 5 leaves to 1 pint of water and add lemon juice and honey to taste.

● *Bruises and sprains*

Apply crushed comfrey leaves directly on to the bruise or sprain. You can also use it in a poultice. In the Middle Ages comfrey was widely used to treat broken bones. Its very name comes from the medieval Latin word *confirma* which points to the widespread belief that comfrey could join together broken bones.

● *Corns*

Put a slice of raw garlic on the corn, cover it with a bandage or plaster and renew it daily until the corn drops off.

● *Cuts and wounds*

If you have yarrow in the garden you can squeeze the juice directly into the cut. Hence some of its many local names: 'soldier's woundwort', 'blood-wort' and 'staunchweed'.

Leaves of St John's Wort (*Hypericum*) can be bandaged on to a cut.

If you're dealing with a small cut, cut a fleshy leaf of a houseleek in half and rub it on the wound to aid healing.

● *Headache*

Teas made from limeflower, elderflower, chamomile, marjoram and mint will all relieve headaches. Prepare them by mixing 1 pint of boiling water to 1 ounce of the herb and leaving the brew to stand for 10–15 minutes.

❂ *Hiccups*

Chew mint leaves.

❂ *Inflammation and ulceration of the gums*

Sage is very effective. Use it either as a tea, or simply chew 1 or 2 fresh leaves from time to time.

Make the tea from ½ ounce of dried sage to 1 pint of boiling water and use it warm as a drink, or cool as a mouthwash.

❂ *Insect bites*

The juice of parsley or basil squeezed directly on to the bite will relieve stinging and swelling. So will the juice of a raw onion or the juice of yarrow.

❂ *Mouthwash*

Half-a-dozen sage leaves mixed with 1 pint of boiling water, infused and strained, makes a mild, refreshing mouthwash.

❂ *Shock*

Either 1 teaspoonful of sage or 2 teaspoonfuls of basil mixed with 1 pint of boiling water will make a herbal tea that drunk freely will help reduce the effects of shock.

❂   *Sleeplessness*

Limeflowers and basil, either on their own or together, make a soothing drink to send you off to sleep. Take 1 teaspoonful of limeflowers or 1/2 teaspoonful of basil to 1 pint of boiling water. Add honey if you like.

Or you could try lemon balm, using 1 ounce of lemon balm to 1 pint of boiling water. Let this infuse and drink it after 10 minutes. It is also a deliciously refreshing summer drink – with ice and a sprig of mint.

❂   *Splinters*

My old stand-by comfrey is marvellous with splinters, too. Crush a few leaves and apply the juice to soothe the discomfort and aid healing.

❂   *Stress and nervousness*

Lemon balm can relieve stress too. This time mix 3 teaspoonfuls to 1 pint of boiling water. Let it stand for, say, 15 minutes, then drink, with honey if you prefer it sweeter.

Clover and marjoram are also good for calming the nerves. I use 1 heaped dessertspoonful of red clover heads and 1/2 a teaspoonful of dried marjoram, mixed with 1 pint of boiling water. Leave this to stand for 15 minutes and once more sweeten it with a little honey, if that's how you like it.

❂   *Tonics*

Not the sort to be mixed with gin – but splendid pick-me-ups all the same. All the following herbal combinations, mixed in proportions of 3 teaspoonfuls to 1 pint of boiling water, are very restorative: dandelion and basil; peppermint and tansy; nettle and lemon balm; or thyme and fennel (1 of thyme to 2 of fennel).

⬢   *Warts*

Apply the milky juice from a dandelion stalk as often as possible over a period of a few days and the wart should disappear.

I think the golden rule with all these remedies (and the same goes for organic gardening) is to be prudent. Don't take a hammer to crack a nut. Try diluting a herbal tea when you take it for the first time. And don't try to get results faster by doubling your intake. In my experience 1 wineglassful taken 3 times a day is sufficient.

Using herbs to make you feel better doesn't stop there. There's nothing quite like a restorative herbal bath to ease your aches and pains after a day toiling in the garden. It seems a fair exchange for all your hard work.

Chamomile, rosemary, horsetail, elder, lavender, marigold, nettle and mint will all add their own special quality to bathtime. I like to make a strong solution and add this to the bath water, or swish one of those perforated tea gadgets filled with dried herbs about in the full, steaming bath. Either way the smell and sensation are richly rewarding.

And when you're out of the bath, cosmetic preparations from your own garden add the ideal finishing touch. Any herbal book will give you masses of ideas; these are some of my own favourites.

● COSMETIC PREPARATIONS

● *Hair lotions and tonics*

Nettle or sage liquid makes a splendid hair lotion.

Rosemary and thyme ($1/2$ ounce of each) mixed with 1 pint of boiling water makes a good hair tonic. Make sure you sieve it well before using.

● *Eye lotion*

A handful of elderflowers mixed with 1 pint of boiling water and allowed to simmer for a few minutes before cooling gives a soothing eye lotion. Make sure it is well sieved before use, by pouring through fine muslin.

● *Skin freshener*

Macerate (soak) 1 cupful of flowers of elder in $3/4$ pints of hot water for 2 hours to give yourself a truly homegrown skin freshener.

● *Lip Balm*

If cold winter winds crack your lips, cold marigold tea will soon have them on the mend. Mix a loose handful of marigolds with 1 pint of boiling water. Calendula cream 'marigold' is available from health shops if nature cannot provide what you need closer to hand.

Finally, when you come down to enjoy a well-earned bite to eat, your herb garden will once more provide all you need for a mouth-watering meal and not just in pinches here and there to improve the lamb or decorate the potatoes – as I hope to show with a few favourite recipes that come later.

The pleasure I gained from growing herbs and my success, modest as it was, at Altrincham, and later in my next garden in nearby Timperley, gave me first-hand experience of a 'different' sort of gardening. From there it was really only a short step to gardening completely organically.

I made the discovery, if I can put it like that, from reading about the Henry Doubleday Research Association (HDRA) in a gardening magazine. The article inspired me to write to them for information at their old headquarters at Bocking in Essex (they're now at Ryton Gardens near Coventry). When I read what they sent back it was as if a veil was lifted from my eyes. For the first time in my gardening life all the various things I'd been trying to do, all the wildlife and natural interests that I had enjoyed since childhood, came together in a beautifully simple and sensible creed.

The herbs, and potions made from them, had started me down the right path, but even then I'd unwittingly use a chemical weedkiller from time to time and in so doing negate so much of the good work that I now realized the herbs and all the other plants were actually doing unseen on my behalf.

Reading what the country's leading organic gardening organization had to say convinced me immediately that this was the direction I'd been nudging towards for so long.

It wasn't world-shattering, but I knew instinctively that it just made perfect sense. I wrote back and became a life member there and then – a card-carrying organic gardener with no looking back, and with no more chemicals into the bargain!

From then onwards gardening for me was to be a simple quest to find natural harmony and balance. It was also going to be the greatest fun – as Andrew Marvell wrote at the end of 'The Garden',

How could such sweet and wholesome hours
Be reckoned, but with herbs and flowers.

2 Planning and Starting a Garden

'As is the garden, such is the gardener.'

Hebrew Proverb

It can be very revealing, a garden. Garden watching is an entertaining pastime when stuck in a slow-moving train, or sitting up top on a bus in heavy traffic. Try it.

It's fun to imagine the owners of the gardens. One thinks that the neatly manicured plots with carefully measured out African marigolds and lobelia belong to people whose furniture is polished every Friday without fail and who change the colour of their toilet rolls to match the soap and towels. Conversely the scrapyard effect of some gardens indicates a similar feckless attitude to life indoors.

Not that this need necessarily be the case. I have known gardeners who spend so much time outside on their beloved acre that their houses are depositories for seed potatoes, smelly bags of unthinkable origin and seedlings galore – there seeming to be no dividing line between house and garden – and certainly no time left in their busy schedules to enjoy hearth and home. Then there are the owners of immaculate, 'not a speck of dust or a thing out of place' homes who run amok when let loose in the garden and revel in joyous abandonment of order. How splendid – how expressive.

As far as my garden goes, I certainly subscribe to the latter school of thought. I thrive on variety and change and I'm also at my happiest in what is best described as ordered muddle. That doesn't mean to say I like things to be dirty or untidy – far from it. But I don't feel totally at ease if everything looks absolutely pristine either. My home is different – I'm a bit 'prissy' indoors.

My present garden is somewhere to be lived in and enjoyed, not a display to be admired from a distance. It must be admitted that when I first made its acquaintance, the garden, with its few fruit trees and roughly cropped grass, did not seem an obvious soulmate. Still, as Lancelot Brown would have said (with justification) it had 'capabilities'.

It was the Dales themselves that carried me away that spring nineteen years ago. I'd visited them from Huddersfield as a child and the image of their wild, rugged beauty had stayed with me. It was soon after Madge Hindle had joined me in the cast of *Coronation Street* that I started spending gloriously happy weekends with her and her husband, Michael, in the Dales and the idea of a home of my own there took root.

It was another dear friend, Russell Harty, who actually discovered one for me. Russell knew the area very well from the days when he had taught at Giggleswick School. He had joined Madge and Michael in buying their house (there was a big barn next to it which Russell had converted for his own use). And we used to enjoy lovely weekend parties with the three of them: drinks with Russell, tottering back for another glorious meal prepared by Michael, who is a stupendously good cook, and invariably ending up singing daft songs around the piano while Russell played. They were always very happy times.

Michael had suggested that I might like to move up to the area, and on one of my weekend visits Russell announced that he had spotted a couple of properties for sale which he thought I'd like. So off we went to view.

Driving up the narrow stony lane to the little group of houses nestling below a majestic hill I had difficulty believing that places as tranquil and remote as this could still be found.

There were two houses for sale. One I mentally ruled out straight away as being beyond my price range. But as the second already had people looking round it, we went back to the first.

Through a gate in the wall we found steps at the gable end of the house which led up to the first floor. The ground floor was being used as garaging, so all the rooms were upstairs, providing magnificent views right over the fields to the distant hills. Outside the house was a lovely terrace laid with local stone which led down to what amounted to a rough field, bounded (in its defence) by dry-stone walls all the way round. Russell loved it and I was almost too excited to speak, except for muffled asides about the price being obviously beyond my reach; though we both knew that I didn't mean it.

When Russell did enquire about the asking price my misgivings proved to be unfounded and a telephone call later the owner accepted my offer. There were ten of us staying with Madge, Michael and Russell that weekend and great were the celebrations!

So great were they that when it came to the following morning and my second visit it took the party some considerable time to assemble. I was awake and ready to go at four. Sleep was impossible. I read. I went for a walk. I came back and still they were all in bed. In the end we didn't get back to the house until eleven, by which time I had difficulty containing my excitement.

My formal offer went in the next day and silence descended, ominously. A day later my solicitor called with the bad news that there'd been so much interest in the house that the owner had decided to put it to open offer. Was I prepared to increase mine? I was deeply disappointed, but had to agree.

The following weekend I went for a third visit, which only confirmed my eagerness. The offer had to be raised once more, we heard from the estate agents. I was chancing my luck, I knew, but my instincts egged me on and we drove into town with the final sealed offer gripped in my fingers. Outside the estate agent's I paused, looked up for some divine intervention before dropping the envelope through the letter box and found it was the wrong office. Never mind the other bidders, I nearly missed the house completely. My little communion with on high had spared me. More to the point my offer was finally accepted and I moved in that summer.

Looking back it's quite hard to imagine the garden as I first started working in it that summer all those years ago. To begin with I was happy to enjoy its simplicity, blending so effortlessly as it did with its environment. However, the grass had to be cut and that would take at least three hours. I never timed it, but friends did and that was how long it took them to cut and rake it all. There was quite a little hillock as well which used to practically kill me as I struggled up and over it.

For a while I was contented, but the monotony

of unbroken mowing and the fact that I missed the plants which had given such pleasure in my gardens in Altrincham and Timperley set me thinking about changes.

The hillock was the first candidate for a facelift, offering itself as the natural location for a rockery. One of my sons was staying for the weekend when the idea came to me and together we removed the turf.

If I've any regrets in my gardening it's that the Good Lord didn't think to match my enthusiasm with equal measures of strength and stature. I wasn't made to build rockeries, and a local contractor was engaged to finish the job for me.

I'd conceived the idea of creating a miniature of the hill that rises behind the house. However, my powers of imagination failed to translate into his and when I got back home to admire his handiwork, three little rings of what looked like pebbles decorated the bald, bare bump that I'd left him to work on. Lesson number one in building a rockery is that you need pretty large stones to achieve the desired result.

Luckily for me one of my neighbours had a digger capable of moving the sort of rocks that should have been used. So Bill, his wife Jackie and I set about creating what felt like a Pharaoh's pyramid at times. There was one rock in particular that had the two women in the gang pushing horizontally like a rugger scrum as we struggled and strained to get it into position. Much later, and after a great deal of effort and giggling, even this whopper was in place with only a small portion showing once the soil had been spread around it. The whole thing was a testament to the kindliness of my neighbours.

For a first attempt at building a rockery I think it worked quite well. I dare say it could be improved, and maybe when the plants get too old it would be a good idea to rebuild it, but that's a job that lies some way in the future. Garden construction work isn't a favourite pastime of mine, though Jo, the organic gardening friend who used to help me, loves it. It seems always to be difficult to find anyone to help with the garden, so I felt very fortunate, in our somewhat remote community, to have found someone like Jo Taylor who is a totally dedicated professional organic gardener – a rarity and heaven sent. She now lives too far away to give me regular help, but answers the call when I need her, as she has a particular affection for my garden.

The success of the rockery set me planning on a broader canvas. Here I was helped by a young couple who'd recently left horticultural college to start up as landscape gardeners.

I knew I didn't want a regimented garden. It had to look as natural as possible – a controlled mess, if you like – something that would blend sympathetically with its totally natural environment. I can't pretend that the garden *is* totally natural, simply because it's full of things that wouldn't grow there in the wild, so I like to think of it as a little oasis.

I've never been a great one for sitting around in the garden. I like to be kept busy. I adore getting filthy and relish the rewarding fatigue that comes from doing hard physical work. Acting on the stage or in the studio demands stamina and energy in its own right, but it is totally different from the labours that Jo and I happily put ourselves to in those early days in the garden. Though I have to admit that she always managed to remain almost spotless while I was the one who ended the day well and truly grubby.

I knew that I wanted variety in the garden too, a good mix of plants that would attract a whole range of wildlife. That's another important organic gardening principle. Making your garden as like a natural habitat as possible goes a long way to introducing the natural predators that can balance the plant damaging species that the garden also attracts.

Apart from those considerations I was keen to create a fluid garden, one that revealed itself to you gradually as opposed to a garden that you could take in at a glance.

So, bearing all of this in mind the two garden designers and I drew up a plan that incorporated the range of borders I wanted, joined by little stepping-stone paths, with a main curving path providing a sinuous link between the terrace at one end and the vegetable garden at the other.

On paper it looked wonderful and while I was away one week they moved in, removed the turf and dug over the bare soil, which must have been jolly hard work with all the stones they unearthed.

Their work had finished when I returned. My new garden was laid out exactly according to plan – and it looked awful!

Left to themselves, my landscapers would have been more tentative in their approach, but I had known what I wanted and they'd carried out my wishes in every detail. Large areas of dry stony earth took on the appearance of a lovingly prepared building site. And what had seemed like a considerable number of shrubs on my planting list cut forlorn isolated figures in the barren wasteland I'd managed to create.

Never would I advise anyone to be as drastic in planning a garden. Not only did it look so bare, the

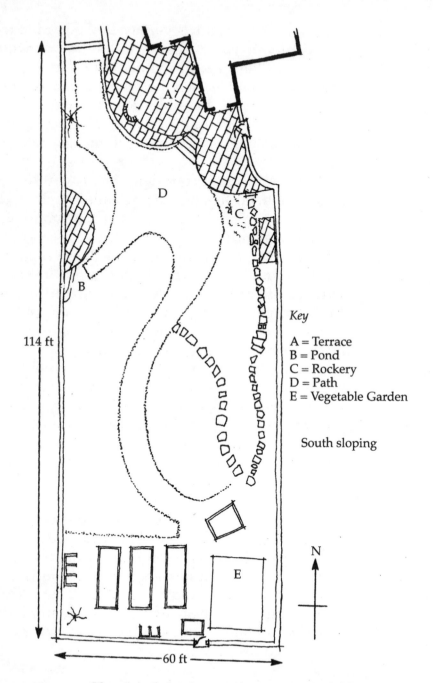

114 ft

60 ft

Key

A = Terrace
B = Pond
C = Rockery
D = Path
E = Vegetable Garden

South sloping

N

The original plan for my organic garden in the Dales

work caused by the weeds that immediately took over could have been utterly demoralizing.

The one piece of professional advice that I did follow was to fill the garden with as many plants as I could afford. I thought I'd been fairly extravagant in buying the ones that they put in for me, but the wide open spaces demanded more and until the plants took root and grew to maturity, the weeds grew thick and fast.

Anyone who was offering plants was welcomed with open arms. I remember putting a card on the Granada studios notice board inviting anyone splitting plants to get in touch, and they did – sometimes with great generosity. Even so it took an age before green replaced brown as the dominant garden colour.

In those early stages it did feel at times as if the garden was enjoying watching me at work rather than the other way round. I started growing vegetables early on and they demanded my attention at the same time as everything else – pounds of peas to be picked and frozen, strawberries to be made into jam – the work piled up and was never-ending.

I don't want to exaggerate what I let myself in for, nor would it be fair to claim that I didn't enjoy making steady progress (most of the time). But after tackling the garden largely on my own, and seeing how terrible it had looked at first, I would advise anyone thinking of wholesale redesigning of their garden seriously to consider how long it will be before it starts to look presentable again and to ask themselves honestly whether they are prepared to put up with that degree of disruption and constant maintenance. Perhaps if I'd been more aware of some of the weed-prevention techniques that I'll be mentioning later I could have made things easier for myself, but then it's in my star sign cheerfully to take on lots of things at once and then find a way of dealing with them all as they pile up and demand attention.

Looking back, I have few regrets. The garden has matured beyond my expectations, while retaining most of its initial structure and design. A few plants were originally sited in the wrong place. Some perennials should have been planted facing south and west when in fact they were planted facing eastwards. Others have died because they weren't suited to the environment. But there were fairly few casualties and a great many rewarding successes.

Garden design is an art about which many mouth-watering books have been written. However, when it comes to the fundamentals of planting, there are a few basic factors which govern your choice. You need to decide whether the plant is suited to your soil; later I'll be mentioning ways of analysing that. You have to consider whether the place where you want it to grow is predominantly sunny or shady. How sheltered is it? How large will the plant grow? Will it be suitable for the size of border you have in mind? What colour are its flowers and foliage and when do they appear? An organic gardener will also want to consider to what extent a plant is resistant to pests and diseases, or whether it attracts any particular species that might usefully prey on pests that could threaten a neighbouring plant.

I didn't really develop my vegetable garden until the main areas of ornamental plants were established and under control, but if you're considering growing fruit and vegetables – and there's nothing to equal the taste of your own, chemical-free, freshly picked produce that's only had to travel the length of the garden from its bed to your kitchen table – then you should plan where to site it at the outset, even if you won't be cultivating vegetables right away. I'll be dealing with this area of the garden later.

You'll want to make space too for a compost heap and possibly a bin in which to make leaf-mould (more of that anon). Neither are features you'll want to look at all the time, so discreet 'screening' or subtle positioning can make a lot of difference to the overall appearance of the garden.

A garden shed is something else you might consider getting, in which case it too will have to be taken into consideration as you sketch out your plans.

My own experience with garden sheds has been mixed, I must say. When I decided the time had come to invest in one, I opted for a metal shed. My brother-in-law had one and seemed to get on with it pretty well. It didn't require the same degree of maintenance as a wooden shed and it appeared to be more robust in general.

What I hadn't bargained for was the condensation and the noise of its sliding door. I can't say its appearance appealed to me much either, but when I discovered that it made a nasty screeching sound whenever I opened or closed the door that put me off completely.

The metal shed and I weren't made for each other and when my builder offered to buy it from me, I jumped at the chance and replaced it with a traditional wooden shed, which looks much more at home. That expensive mistake taught me that buying garden equipment of any sort needs care and forethought.

⚘ GARDEN TOOLS

When I started gardening I kitted myself out by buying the basic tools at an auction. Chosen with care these can still give years of good service at a fraction of the cost of new tools.

What's really important about any garden tool is that it should be efficient and comfortable to use. That means it should be sturdy, sharp (if it's meant to be sharp), well-balanced and suited to your size and shape. If you happen to be my size this is particularly important. Struggling with a full-sized spade would exhaust me in an hour, but armed with a smaller border spade I can keep working from dawn till dusk.

All of this advice has come together in my own tool shed in the form of the stainless steel tools to which I am gradually treating myself. These are the Rolls-Royces of garden tools and it took me years of gardening before I decided to splash out on my first one, but they certainly put routine, heavy garden work in a different perspective.

Until I tried one I wouldn't have believed the difference stainless steel could make to a simple operation like digging. Now I'm a complete convert – the blade slices through the soil so easily compared to my old spade.

I was so thrilled with my stainless steel spade that I bought one for a friend's sixtieth birthday and the first time she used it she was on the phone, almost ecstatic at the difference it was going to make to her gardening. Tools that are a pleasure to use encourage you to keep them clean and return them to the tool shed looking bright and shiny.

I'm not terribly good at sharpening things, which is why I appreciate stainless steel I suppose. But any spade will be easier to use if it's kept sharp and if the blade is put away clean.

Stainless steel tools are certainly a luxury and I don't think I would feel easy about buying them if gardening wasn't my principal hobby. Jo, too, has a few stainless steel tools, but then she gardens professionally, which is a further recommendation I suppose. Provided that any tool is well-made and looked after it will give years of good service.

For anyone starting to garden and wanting to buy the basic tools, I would advise getting the following:

> Spade
> Fork
> Hand trowel
> Hand fork
> Hoe
> Knife
> Secateurs
> Garden rake

I've already mentioned the first four on the list and here are some thoughts about some others.

❁ *Hoe*

There are now lots of different hoes on the market, but I've always been happy using a traditional draw hoe. I also bought one from the HDRA which has a swivelling blade that makes it efficient working both forwards and backwards. In the case of both of these I've had them fitted with handles shorter than the standard length, which makes them more comfortable for someone of my height.

❁ *Knife*

I always keep a little penknife in my pocket when I'm gardening. I got this from the HDRA too. It has a single blade and a wooden handle with a single locking ring and it's always coming in useful.

❁ *Secateurs*

Here again I've treated myself; I have a pair of sprung secateurs with a rotating handle, which can be used comfortably in either hand. I find them very easy to use.

❁ *Rakes*

In addition to the normal garden rake for working the soil, I have a springy lawn rake which does almost constant battle keeping the moss at bay. The dampness in the Dales provides an ideal environment for moss. It looks beautiful all over the drystone walls, but it's less appealing when it invades the grass and just about everything else. We've found that if we don't control the moss in the rockery it creeps into all the surrounding plants, becoming a dreadful tangly problem eventually.

Raking the grass regularly helps reduce the moss but it will never be the complete answer. Recently I asked at Ryton Gardens if they could suggest an organic method of dealing with it and they advised me to keep on working at improving the condition of the soil, particularly the drainage. As with so many aspects of organic gardening, if you get the soil in really good condition, lots of problems will fade away. So I'm improving the soil frantically – and still raking like mad – and as the humus has started to build up over the years and the soil has started to drain better, there are signs of the moss retreating. I live in hope.

❀ *Sieve*

I wouldn't regard this as a priority, but I find a sieve very useful when planting things like carrots, which need a fine, fine tilth. I've still got the sieve I bought originally in an auction years ago. It's an old, battered thing, but it still works.

With soil like mine a sieve is especially useful in removing all the little stones. If you try to grow carrots in soil as stony as this, they often fork. That goes for many of the root crops and I suppose the vegetable bed is the one we tend to sieve most, but it is also beneficial to plant seeds in very fine soil.

❀ *Edging shears*

Whatever the size of the lawn it will always look neat and cared for if the edges are kept well trimmed with a pair of edging shears. These aren't essential either, but they're a nice optional extra.

● *Wheelbarrow*

Before buying my last wheelbarrow, I spent ages investigating what's available. For a long time we used a roller-ball barrow which I like very much because it's light and I can lift it up and down steps if I need to move it to a different level (the drop from the terrace to the garden is a good five feet).

If, however, you are quite tall you might find that your feet kick against the ball when you roll it along, which can be very tiresome. (This detail shows why it's so important to spend a bit of time trying out the feel of any garden tool before you buy it.) It may sound like buying a bed, but if you're going to be using it almost as often, surely it's worth the effort?

● *Post hole borer and lump hammer*

These may seem an odd couple to include, but for us they're indispensable! The ground is so stony that without them getting a stake, or even a cane, into the ground would be next to impossible.

To digress a moment – I throw the stones over the gate at the end of the garden, so that Ernest or Michael, my neighbouring farmers, can take them away to use as infill in their stone walling. When they haven't been to collect them for a while, the heap that's built up is both remarkable and a revealing testament to what my plants have to contend with below the surface.

● *Pickaxe*

This may also come as a surprise, but I've got a pickaxe specifically for prising stones out of the ground. I once bent a good fork trying to do just that and it taught me not to be so stupid again. Ever since, I've tried to discipline myself to use the right tool for the right job and when it comes to some of my stones the pickaxe is undoubtedly the right tool!

I hate giving up on a job and one stone I hit against had me struggling and straining on and off for well over a year. In the end, my friend with the digger offered to lend a hand and when his huge machine finally wrested the stone from the ground it turned out to be over five feet wide! I could have been there till Doomsday hacking away ineffectively with my pickaxe.

● *Tree loppers*

I don't get on frightfully well with my long-handled tree loppers because you need to be quite strong to use them, but they're the only answer to high-level pruning. They just seem to taunt me with another reason for being that little bit stronger.

Tree lopping was rather a painful subject at home a few years ago. I decided the time had come to take the top out of a conifer growing at the far end of the garden; and looked at from ground level it made a great improvement. However, as soon as I went upstairs inside the house, I realized that I'd forgotten to check first what it would look like from there. The answer was that it looked terrible. If ever there was an example of disastrous pruning my poor conifer fitted the bill. Fortunately it recovered reasonably quickly and I have planted a clematis Frances Rivers to grow through it, but I'm really quite ashamed of my stupidity, and now check the possible results of pruning before I take action.

❀ Shears

There isn't a lot of hedging in my garden, but a pair of hand shears does keep some of the evergreens tidy. At Altrincham and Timperley I had an electric hedge trimmer, not that I ever felt completely at ease with it, nor I suspect did my hedge if the results of some of my 'trimming' were anything to go by.

❀ Lawnmower

For many years I found a small electric Flymo quite adequate. It was easy to use and, used with a special socket that cuts off the current instantly if we accidentally sever the cable, it seems completely safe too. My mower doesn't collect the grass, but provided it isn't too long you can leave the cuttings on the lawn to fertilize it. They disappear and break down quickly, so this isn't as untidy as it may sound and the cuttings save you from having to add other fertilizers during the main growing season. Now I have turned some of the planting areas over to grass, a motor mower is the best option.

● *Half-moon edging tool*

This isn't an essential tool either. We find it useful for keeping the edges of beds neat. It's also handy for cutting turf if you need to patch an area of lawn.

● *Hosepipe and watering can*

I'm lucky living in an area where we have enough rainfall still to allow the use of garden hoses. For ten years I ran a hose from a tap right by the house, but I've finally got round to installing a water supply in the lower level of the garden to save battering my plants every time I want to do some watering. Crossing the terrace, as it used to, the hose would knock over the herbs, bash against the plants growing on the wall below the terrace and then push against plants in the beds as it was moved around.

To go with my hosepipe I've got a sprinkler on a tripod which gives the plants the closest watering to natural rainfall that I've ever come across. Using a really good thick mulch helps retain early season moisture in the soil, but I'm still surprised how much water plants need in summer. I also have a device that lets me spray a foliar feed, or other organic liquid treatment, on to specific plants, and I do find this extremely useful.

The watering can fitted with a fine rose comes into its own when you only have a little watering to do, a few pots perhaps, or something specific that doesn't require unreeling the hose and carefully threading it to its destination. My latest addition in the vegetable garden is a perforated hose watering system which I use on a timer, and it has made a considerable improvement, particularly in dry spells.

Marcia Warren, a friend of many years and an actress I admire enormously, has other skills – she's a clever gardener too. As she sometimes has to be away from home for a few days, she fills empty wine bottles with water and inserts them upside-down in pots of terrace plants. The theory is that the water will gradually seep into the compost, thus preventing a total dry-out.

❁ *Gloves*

I always set off gardening wearing gloves, though they're not always on when I return after a day's work. They do protect your hands, that's for sure. But having small hands I find a lot of gloves are too big and cumbersome. The arrangement that suits me best is to wear a pair of rubber gloves or what look like surgical gloves inside a pair of light-weight cotton ones, those with little rubber bobbles on the fingers to help you grip things. For heavy stone-heaving I try to manage with the big tough gloves, but they aren't totally satisfactory. In summer I sometimes wear the cotton gloves under the rubber gloves, and in winter – fine thermals.

❁ *Shredder*

I've left mentioning the shredder until last, because it's the one gardening tool I've acquired over which a question mark hangs in my mind.

I should say that I like the idea behind the shredder; that's why I bought it. But I wonder how economical it is in its use of electricity, and the environmental implications which come with that consumption of energy, in order to get a few bags of chopped-up garden waste for use on the compost heap or as a mulch.

On the occasions when I've used it with two or three other people I've seen it in a more favourable light. If there's someone to hand over the twiggy, prickly cuttings to be shredded, someone to feed them into the machine and someone to collect the shredded material then I'm sure it's more satisfactory. Trying to use it on my own I find it less successful, very noisy and constantly getting jammed with twiggy bits.

I also find that it isn't essential in the making of my compost, as you will shortly discover.

❀ WASTE NOT, WANT NOT

As I never tire of repeating, organic gardening can be wonderfully thrifty. As a lead-in to ideas I suggest throughout the book, here is a list of things which might otherwise be thrown away, but for which I hope you'll now find further uses in the garden.

Garden waste	on the compost heap
Kitchen waste	on the compost heap
Plastic food containers	slug traps and planters
Net curtains	draped over soft fruit bushes to deter birds
Second-hand timber	for making compost bins, raised beds and stakes
Clear plastic bottles	slug traps, fruit-fly traps and mini-cloches
Old wine bottles	watering pot plants steadily over a few days

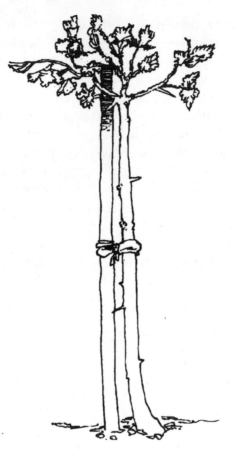

Old tights recycled into tree ties

Plastic yoghurt cartons and liquid soap bottles	cut into strips for plant labels
Newspaper (tabloid)	replacing peat pots
Newspaper and cardboard	mulching (when well weighted down)
Carpet	mulching
Black plastic	mulching
Old tights	tying trees to stakes
Old shower certains	drag mats for collecting prunings, leaves etc

Grapefruit halves	slug deterrents
Holly leaves	slug deterrents
Pine needles	slug deterrents
Hair clippings	slug deterrents
Sand	slug deterrents
Stones	to weigh down branches of fruit trees – and to cover my slug traps.

It's revealing how often slugs feature here. On with the struggle!

3   *Basic Organic Skills*

'Back to earth, the dear green earth.'

William Wordsworth
'Peter Bell', prologue

One of my simplest but constantly rewarding pleasures in the garden is making compost. Now, that may not sound much to shout about, but the successful conversion of sackfuls of kitchen and garden rubbish into this rich, deliciously crumbly, sweet-smelling, soil-enhancing humus combines many of the principles that makes organic gardening my particular creed.

Making compost is a perfect way to recycle what is often seen as rubbish. It's one of the most natural ways of conserving the natural materials we're eager to make use of and frequently just as willing to squander. A gardener who makes and uses compost puts something back into the garden and replenishes the nutrients that give health and life to his or her plants. Then there's the bonus that the regular addition of compost year on year steadily improves the soil with all the benefits to plants that follow. Compost is such a vital part of successful organic gardening, and one that will feature regularly throughout the book, that I want to mention it right away, together with what I regard as other fundamental organic 'skills'.

I have to admit that Jo and I didn't entirely see eye to eye on how compost should be made. (And judging by the wide variety of compost-making containers that are available, nor do many gardeners far more experienced than we are!) All I can say is that both our methods, thoroughly carried out, have produced very usable and nutritious compost for several years.

In the end a lot depends on how you want your compost 'heap' to look while it steadily goes about its good work. After all, it's going to be there for at least six months through the winter, and from three to four months in the summer. The finished product may be sensational but you don't want the 'heap' to be an eyesore in the garden.

For all its natural benefits, making compost in the garden is our way of speeding up what nature takes far longer to do left to her own devices. By bringing together a large amount of organic material into a confined space, a compost heap produces the heated environment in which thrive the micro-organisms that break down animal and vegetable waste. The heat generated by this process (and it can reach 140°F (60°C)) has the added benefit of killing weeds, and any seeds and diseased material that may have slipped in by accident. As a result, a pile of carefully prepared garden rubbish and selected kitchen waste can be transformed in a comparatively short time into something immensely useful and highly beneficial.

So, having whetted your appetite, if I can put it like that, this is what you do.

✿ COMPOSTING MATERIALS

These depend on what you have available, but it's important to get a good balance no matter what you use.

Firstly some things that I *don't* put on to my compost heap:

✿ *Hard twiggy material*

I know this can have its benefits but I find it awful to remove when I get down to the bottom of the heap and all the little bits are mixed up with the lovely crumbly compost. If you do include these in a compost heap they need to be well cut up into little pieces (and you'll know my thoughts on mechanical shredders by now), or bashed with a hammer to 'soften' them up.

✿ *Meat, fat, fish and bones*

These can attract rodents and they'd certainly attract cats given half a chance, which would cause such a mess. I expect these ingredients would make the compost heap a bit smelly too, which is certainly something to be avoided as far as I'm concerned.

✿ *Perennial weed roots, seedheads and diseased material*

In principle a well-made compost heap should generate enough heat to destroy these, but as I'm fortunate enough to have quite a lot of other material to use, I prefer not to take the risk that they might not be killed off in the composting process.

Now for the things that I *do* put in my compost heap:

> All kitchen vegetable and fruit waste
> Tea leaves
> Coffee grounds
> Egg shells
> Grass mowings (mine haven't been treated with a weedkiller, but chemically treated mowings should be avoided)
> Manure
> Straw
> Bracken
> Nettles
> Comfrey
> Yarrow
> Windfalls
> Wood ash
> Spent potting compost
> Hair clippings
> Sawdust
> Soil
> Animal and bird manure
> Shredded newspaper

The key to successful compost making is to get a good mixture of materials. It might be very tempting to rely on, perhaps, grass mowings alone (if you're still collecting them in the grass box rather than letting them fertilize the lawn), but a mass of grass mowings will turn into a sticky, slimy mess. You could dig this into the ground, but you couldn't call it compost.

No, the secret is to get a balance between

carbon materials and nitrogen materials, as well as a good blend of moisture and air. Get the mixture right and your compost heap will have the right amount of air, the right nutritional balance and the right environment in which the compost-making micro-organisms can flourish and multiply.

As any authority will tell you, the best compost heaps are made at one go. The snag with this is that it isn't always possible to have all the ingredients in the right quantities at the right time. You *can* half-build a compost heap, adding to it and completing it before the original material loses its heat, but I prefer to make mine all in one go. To do this I collect my material in large fertilizer sacks. I don't mind admitting that they can look untidy (I'm working on that!) but the end result makes up for any visual detractions they may cause.

I made my best compost heap ever in less than an hour, aided by Joan, my gardening friend from Bristol. We were actually waiting for a couple of other friends to arrive and set to on the spur of the moment. I had all the bags of waste to hand and we worked like Trojans for three-quarters of an hour until we had a splendid heap about four and a half feet high, nicely mixed and covered over with a piece of old carpet to keep in the warmth. Within about four days it had shrunk to about half that height, and you could tell it was really hot inside. The weather was ideal, warm without being too dry. And the combination of materials produced the nicest compost I've ever made.

Jo and I have experimented with various mixtures. I don't have a compost recipe as such but I've found that a mixture based on layers like these works well.

I've listed them in the order in which I would

pile them in the heap. In other words the bottom layer comes first:

Soft twiggy material	8 inches
Thin layer of soil	2 inches
Grass clippings	
(good source of nitrogen)	3 inches
Kitchen waste	8 inches
Nettles or comfrey	
(good source of nitrogen)	3 inches
Manure	
(good source of nitrogen)	5 inches
Wood ash	A sprinkling

Once you've sprinkled your wood ash, you start again, repeating the order until the heap reaches its finished height of between four and five feet. You'll then want some form of covering to keep the heat in, while letting out any excess moisture or gases that build up. Old carpet is marvellous as a compost 'blanket'; sacks and even plastic sheeting punctured here and there work well too.

The order I've given isn't essential and what you put on the heap obviously depends on what you have available. The important point is to change the material every few inches, so that you get a really good mix in which all the different micro-organisms can work their magic.

Getting the right moisture level needn't present a great problem either. In very dry weather the heap can be watered as you build it. In wetter weather using a greater amount of dry material will help balance out the damper conditions.

On the subject of moisture, there's a lot to be said for human urine as a compost activator. So, if you can persuade your gentlemen friends to take a

The garden – as I first saw it.

The scene of desolation – stones and bare earth – what had I done!

The rockery beginning to flourish.

The garden beginning to take shape, with the first year of the
vegetable garden at the bottom.

How it looks today.

The battle nearly won, the plants taking over, the ground cover almost complete.

The wooden shed – so much more sympathetic than its metal predecessor – with the oil tank screened by tumbling roses and Jerusalem artichokes in the foreground.

New Zealand boxes with the leafmould cage – all constructed by Jo.

Hoverfly-attracting poached egg plants in the herb garden with a deep mulch of mushroom compost.

Hedgehog box – 'Des. res. in secluded country setting'.

The 'pool area' with bird bathing facilities conveniently adjacent!

Butterflies attracted to *Sedum spectabile*.

stroll down the garden on a dark evening they can do their bit to help out as well!

As I've already said, there are various ways of actually containing a compost heap, so let me start with the ones that I have used.

There are three general rules that apply to whichever sort of heap you settle on. Build your heap directly on the ground, so that earthworms can work their way into it, to make their own contribution. Be sure to fork over the ground lightly before starting to make the heap; this helps surplus moisture drain away and it makes life a little easier for the worms as they work their way upwards. And remember that you will need to turn your heap when the initial heating has taken place. I'll say more about this in a moment, but it may have some bearing on the sort of container you settle on, and where you put it in the garden.

● *Wire-netting compost bin*

For several years I used a compost bin made of wire netting lined with insulation material. (The wire netting isn't suitable on its own because it allows the heat to escape; cardboard, paper, or straw provide the required insulation.)

Wire-netting bins have two big advantages: they're easy to build and they're cheap to build.

The size of the bin depends on how much compost you can realistically expect to make. Bearing in mind that compost needs to generate heat, bigger bins tend to be more successful than smaller ones.

Square or rectangular bins are straightforward to make, and keep the 'heap' tidy. For most gardeners a bin measuring 3 feet high by 3 feet wide by 3 feet deep serves their purpose. (For the metrically minded that's approximately 1 metre, by 1 metre, by 1 metre.)

The wire-netting bin needs four upright posts made from stout timber. A layer of wire is stapled round the outside. A second layer is stapled to the inside and the insulation material of cardboard, paper or straw is stuffed between them like the filling of a sandwich. Designing the bin so that the front can be removed makes it possible to dig out the compost when it is ready without having to take apart the whole bin. It's as well to think about this before you start filling the bin!

A protective sloping lid to keep off rain and direct sunlight will help maintain the right balance of moisture.

Apart from being cheap and easy to make, wire-netting bins are light and easy to move around the garden. However, they don't last for ever. In fact the insulation material will rot down as the compost forms. You have to watch the type of wire netting you use too. It needs to be well galvanized or coated in plastic if it isn't going to rust.

I was perfectly happy with my wire-netting bin to begin with, but as my enthusiasm for compost has grown I've looked for something more substantial and permanent.

❂ Compost heaps

Here I should say a word about compost heaps, as opposed to bins.

I suppose my only misgiving is that I never seem able to build a heap that stays tidy. Mine always seem to end up as rather scruffy mounds.

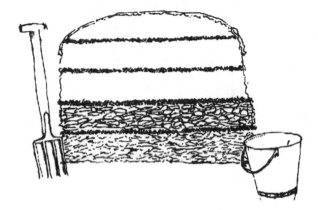

Compost heap

The principle of mixing materials in layers applies just the same. For stability you should begin with a bottom layer measuring at least 6 feet by 4 feet, gradually tapering the layers that you pile on top, so that the finished heap, 4 feet high, looks something like the flat-topped pyramids that were built in ancient Mexico. If this is covered with a sheet of black polythene it will help retain the moisture inside and prevent it from becoming waterlogged by heavy rain.

● *New Zealand boxes*

When it came to creating a new bin in my garden Jo and I agreed that we couldn't better a New Zealand box; since she was going to build it, I wasn't going to stand in her way.

The New Zealand box, which was invented by the New Zealand Compost Society, has all the

New Zealand boxes and leaf cage

features of the best compost bins, as a result of which it is a bit more complex and expensive to build than other homemade ones. However, anyone handy with ruler, saw and hammer should be able to make one, and once built your New Zealand box will last for years.

As the drawing shows, it's a wooden structure shaped like the letter E; one of its main attractions is that it gives you *two* bins.

It's worth taking a little care in making a compost bin that could give you good service for upwards of twenty years. If you plan to move your bin around the garden, or if you think you might want to take it with you if you move house, you'll find both of these easier if you build the bin with sides that can be bolted together.

The corner posts are about 2 inches square. To these are nailed the planks made from toughish wood, probably 9 inches wide and half an inch thick for durability. (There's no need to go out and buy new timber for this job. Good second-hand timber from a reclamation yard will do just as well – provided it is cheaper. Jo and I were amazed to find out that a load of second-hand timber we had delivered was *more expensive* than new timber!)

Fit the planks closely together to form solid sides. This prevents the outside layers from drying out too much and also helps to keep in the heat; wood is a good insulator. There should also be a sloping lid which can be constructed out of the same planks and so can the individual ones that fit into the slots to form the easily removable front. Don't forget the piece of old carpet or hessian, cut to size, that sits on top of the compost to insulate it.

Now for the second bin. This is for turning the compost and with the New Zealand box it's simply a matter of turning the compost from one bin into the other. This makes the job easier and keeps the whole operation tidy.

❂ *Other types of compost bin*

There are quite a number of different types of compost bin on the market. They range in size, complexity and durability. You'll be able to judge for yourself whether or not a ready-made bin will suit your needs. Though you should consider: whether or not it is the right size (is it big enough to hold the material you'll have available?); is easy to put together and use; and is strong enough to last the test of time.

I've seen some compost bins that make a feature of turning the compost regularly, rather like huge egg-timers. These certainly help to get lots of air into the 'heap' and consequently the contents stay hot for longer than in conventional 'heaps'. But once it has cooled, it needs to be unloaded to allow the compost to mature.

Back to the D-I-Y bins: you can build permanent bins from bricks or concrete blocks, though you'll need to make sure that air can penetrate either of these from the bottom. On the other hand very serviceable short-term bins can be made from simply piling straw bales together to form a square C, or the E shape of the New Zealand box.

❂ *Turning compost*

The process of turning is to compost what the secondary fermentation is to champagne, if I can put it like that. Turning stimulates a secondary heating process which gets all the micro-organisms going again just when they think the job is done.

In practical terms, turning takes place about a week after the heap starts to cool. By this time the contents will have reduced significantly. If you have two bins you simply fork it from one into the other. If you're using a heap, you take it apart and rebuild it. In either case the outside material needs to go to the inside to ensure that it is exposed to the heat and micro-organic activity. Turning lets air into the 'heap' and gives the micro-organisms inside the supply of oxygen they need to get working once more. Turning also gives you the chance to add water if the heap is too dry or to improve the balance of materials if there seems to be, say, too much woody material.

However, don't be disheartened if, when you examine your fresh compost at the end of the process, you do find material that hasn't completely decomposed. This is never wasted. In fact, it can be a very useful starter for the next heap.

● LEAFMOULD

Leafmould is wonderful stuff and I use lots in my garden, but it does take much longer to break down than compost. As this, the whole process of rotting down and decomposition, takes place the leaves slowly release their nutrients back into the soil, replenishing what they have taken to grow. This is what makes leafmould such a valuable soil improver and conditioner. The way the leafmould is formed is actually quite different from that in which garden compost is made, which is why it's a good idea to have a separate bin specifically for housing your fallen leaves.

We collect ours in the autumn and pile them inside a wire netting cage, which again measures about 3 feet high by 3 feet wide by 3 feet deep.

The cage helps to keep them tidy. A leafmould heap never generates the level of heat found in a garden compost heap, so you don't have to be so concerned about insulation. Leafmould heaps don't need turning either, nor do they depend on nitrogen-rich activators to the same extent as compost heaps.

You can use most types of leaves, though it is as well to avoid using evergreen leaves like holly and conifer needles. The best leafmould is made from leaves with a high tannin content, leaves like oak and beech.

The leaves can be well trodden in until the cage is full. Watering dry leaves will help the rotting down process, otherwise the job is finished as far as the gardener is concerned. Just exercise a little patience and in a year's time the leafmould will be ready to dig in. If you want finer potting compost, you'll have to leave the leafmould for two, or even three, years.

We usually remove our cage after a year and leave the heap to carry on rotting down while we start a fresh one for that year's fall.

For smaller quantities you can use plastic sacks punctured with holes.

It's tempting to consider asking your local authority for some of the tons of leaves that it has to clear away every autumn but there are hidden (and not so hidden) risks with sources like these. Apart from the obvious hazards posed by dogs and litter, some leaves gathered from streets may contain quite high levels of lead and other substances from the emissions of passing traffic which you certainly wouldn't want to introduce into the garden. Having said that, if you can find a reliable source you could do your garden and someone else a very useful service.

If patience isn't your particular virtue you can speed up the process of making leafmould by adding spring grass cuttings to about a quarter of the volume of the leaves. Use the cuttings in spring when there is less chance of weed seeds being included. If these are mixed in with the leaves they will produce a cross between compost and leafmould inside a year.

Making leafmould is another splendid example of turning what so many gardeners see as a nuisance into something enormously beneficial and useful. The process doesn't take much effort: whatever time is spent gathering the leaves is more than repaid by the plant foods that are returned to the soil.

The great disappointment is that lots of gardeners spend just as much time collecting leaves only to burn them on a bonfire. I've already indicated the waste that this represents, but it has more serious implications. Bonfires, particularly the smouldering, slow-burning kind, can pose a potential health hazard from the gases they give off, quite apart from their environmental threat and the nuisance they can be to neighbours.

If you have to light a bonfire to dispose of woody materials that can't be composted, go for a dry, quick-burning fire that consumes the material rapidly without producing palls of noxious, carcinogenic smoke. Keep as much of the material to be burnt dry and add this to the fire as it starts to blaze; don't just shove some kindling into the base of the pile and hope for the best. Before you even light it, check that nothing has taken up residence in what you're about to set fire to. Hedgehogs, the gardener's great friends, particularly enjoy the shelter provided by a convenient stack of branches. So always check first that there's nothing tucked away underneath.

● MANURE

Living in the country, very near a farm where the animals still live close to nature, I am very lucky in having a ready source of farmyard manure. In fact I get almost ecstatic when the farmer brings me a load of muck. When this is delivered it is still too raw to be used directly on plants, which it might damage. It needs to be covered over to prevent the rain from washing away its nutrients and to give it time to rot down to a rich, brown material that will be ready for the garden in about twelve months' time.

Not all farmyard manure comes as free from chemicals as mine. Manure from intensive pig and poultry units may well contain traces of antibiotics and other feed additives which you would probably wish to avoid. That's why it's always wise to check the source of your manure before it's delivered.

Stable manure has always been popular with gardeners, but many horses are now kept on wood shavings or sawdust which take far longer to break down than the traditional stabling material, namely straw. This will also need covering and time to rot down to its most usable dark brown state.

I also am a great fan of mushroom compost. When I gardened at Timperley I had bags and bags of this delivered and was thrilled with it. We use it in the Dales with as much enthusiasm, but not without caution. You have to check carefully whether or not the mushroom compost you so covet has been treated with pesticides. You don't want your good clean earth to be polluted after all your hard work, do you?

If all this talk of compost seems a little un-lady-like, perhaps these few lines will help to show how organic gardening has broadened my mind!

I always experienced a whiff of
   distaste
When anyone talked about
   'animal waste'.

But since I have gardened
Much worse words are
    pardoned;
I'd repeat them – but frankly
    I'm far too shamefaced.

4 Improving the Soil

'Of the earth we make loam.'

William Shakespeare
Hamlet

The answer, as they say, lies in the soil – and in the case of organic gardening that couldn't be more true. There are no temptingly simple chemical fertilizers and pesticides lurking in the potting shed. In their absence the vitality and success of the organic gardener's plants rely on his or her own efforts to enhance and improve the soil with nutrients that are natural to it.

This needn't be as daunting as it sounds. The visible improvement in plants, and the garden in general, that comes each year as the soil is gradually enriched, is ample reward for the time and effort spent in nurturing and nourishing it.

When I gardened at Altrincham, and later at Timperley, I was blessed with some of the best soil any gardener could wish for. Rich, dark and crumbly, it would grow almost anything.

That certainly isn't true of my garden in the Dales, where the soil is basically poor, very stony and predominantly clay. Even so, the regular addition of compost, leafmould, manure, mulches and organic fertilizers has brought about a steady improvement. My worms will vouch for that. When I moved in they were pale, undernourished and thin on (and in) the ground. Today, I can proudly boast, they're sleek, well-rounded and bursting with health – worms to be proud of. There are also masses of them. The garden is teeming with life out of sight beneath my feet.

These are the visible signs of soil improvement; the encouraging glimpses that show you you're helping to leave your little patch of earth in better condition than you found it.

I don't want to give the misleading impression that this comes about without any effort. I've got nineteen years of struggling with clay and what seems to have amounted to a small mountain of laboriously collected stones to bear witness to what's involved. But I do want to show that everything you do to improve your soil can, quite literally, bear fruit.

Perhaps I should also make the point that the 'soil' in which garden plants grow is the upper eight inches or so of topsoil. The subsoil that lies below contains a few valuable trace nutrients, but none of the rich organic matter and nutrients which gives topsoil its distinctive quality. As far as possible the two should always be kept apart during cultivation.

So, how do you set about improving the soil?

Not being a chemist, a biologist or any sort of scientific '-ist', I am happy to rely on tried and tested methods that make sense to me.

The first of these is to find out what sort of soil you have. This may seem obvious. But try growing plants that aren't suited to it and you'll soon discover the disappointment of overlooking this elementary first step.

There are half a dozen broadly accepted types of soil, and you can get a good idea which category yours falls into by feeling it; by talking to neighbours who've been gardening it for several years; and, if you're good at spotting wild flowers, by noticing which trees and plants are growing well on it.

● TYPES OF SOIL

A simple hand test can tell you a lot about the soil's structure. Pick a small handful, moisten it and see if you can roll it into a ball. If it feels gritty and refuses to roll into a neat sphere the soil is sandy.

Now try rubbing the surface of the ball. If you can rub it smooth, there's a high proportion of clay. If the surface still remains slightly coarse the soil is probably silt.

Next try the sausage test. Can your soil roll into a sausage? If it falls apart again, you'll know that it's sandy. If it does form a sausage, it's got a high clay content.

Finally try to see if you can bend the sausage. If it bends a little and then breaks, that's a sign of silt. But if it bends without difficulty and stays in shape, you'll know for certain that your soil is clay.

● *Clay*

A lot of gardeners almost despair at the mention of clay. Clay seems to promise little but hours of back-breaking digging, only to be rewarded by a rock-hard, cracked surface in dry summers and a sticky, unworkable morass in winter.

What many of them overlook is that clay is usually wonderfully fertile. It's the tight bonding of its small particles, causing it to drain badly, which makes clay soil so unworkable. This structure also causes clays to take longer to warm in spring than lighter soils, which means that sowing has to take place later than would be the case with the sort of soil that I had in Altrincham, for example. Given the right treatment, however, clay soils can be broken down. Their tightly-knit structure can be opened up to allow better drainage and the plant foods locked inside can be released to repay you handsomely for your pains.

❂ Sand

By contrast, sandy soils have much larger particles than clay soils. That's what makes them light and easy to work. But a very sandy soil is no more ideal in a garden than a very heavy clay soil. Sandy soils drain very easily, and therefore require a great deal of watering in dry weather. The ease with which they drain also means that most nutrients are easily washed away before plants have a chance to benefit from them. As well as watering, sandy soils require regular feeding.

❂ Loam

This is every gardener's dream, a balanced mixture of clay and sand. Loam is open enough to drain well, but not so open that it loses moisture too rapidly; it is also rich in nutrients. Needless to say, very few soils ever reach this perfect harmony. Clay loam shows a predominance of clay particles, sandy loam a higher density of sand particles.

❁ *Chalk*

Chalk soils often suffer from being very shallow and from drying out quickly. They can also be very stony. Regular doses of organic matter like manure or compost will help bring them into a more usable condition.

❁ *Peat*

Peat soils may sound promising, but they lack some of the nutrients found in other more fertile soils. They are, however, easy to work and given tender loving care will grow a wide variety of plants.

❁ *Silt*

Silty soils share many of the less appealing qualities of clay. They are heavy, drain badly and are easily packed down to form a hard crust. Generous helpings of organic matter will help break down this compact structure, improving drainage and overall fertility.

❁ ACID OR ALKALINE?

There's another straightforward test that will also reveal important information about your soil and, with luck, will save you the frustration and disappointment of trying to grow unsuitable plants in it. This is the test which shows the acid/alkaline balance.

Before dealing with the actual analysis, which takes the form of a pH soil testing kit that you can pick up in garden centre, nursery, or chemist, a quick word might be useful to distinguish between the two types of soil.

❂ *Acid soil*

In gardening terms, the difference amounts to the presence or absence of lime. Acid soils have only a small quantity of lime. Alkaline soils have quite a lot of lime.

Lime supplies calcium, and since worms require calcium they're not terribly keen on acid soils. Bearing in mind the vital role that worms play in improving the soil, it's obviously important to make the soil more attractive to them.

Many of the micro-organisms that contribute to a fertile, easily workable soil don't like high concentrations of acidity either. So on both these counts increasing the proportion of lime is necessary and this can be done quite easily by adding it to the soil, as I'll come to in a moment.

Acid soils also release their nutrients more easily than alkaline soils. This sounds an advantage, but what often happens is that nutrients are released when there are no plants to benefit from them; in this case they are washed away and lost. Once more, improving the level of calcium helps to restrict nutrient release to a more controlled rate.

❂ *Alkaline soil*

Alkaline soils have a lot going for them. They have beneficial levels of lime. They hold on to nutrients better than acid soils do. Worms and valuable micro-organisms love them and a wide range of plants grows well on them, too.

However, there are certain plants that don't like alkaline soils one little bit; heathers, azaleas and rhododendrons are common examples and there are many others. So it's important to check the sort of soil plants like before you hand over your money and rush home to bed them in.

The other negative feature of alkaline soils is that there is very little a gardener can do to alter a high lime concentration. Manure and other organic material may have some effect in time, but there is no corresponding answer to the addition of lime to acid soils.

● *pH testing*

The full pH scale runs from 1 (very strongly acid) to 14 (very strongly alkaline). Perfect balance, or neutrality, is reached with number 7. The gardener is only really concerned with pH numbers that range from 4.5 (very acid soils) to 8.5 (very alkaline ones). Apparently the acid in a car battery has a pH of about 2.

If you want a detailed professional soil analysis, there are laboratories who will perform this for you. Most gardeners, and I'm certainly one of them, can get a useful idea by following the instructions of the D-I-Y soil testing kit that's generally available.

To use this, samples of soil are collected from different parts of the garden, from a depth of about 4 inches. Each sample is left to dry and then each one tested separately in a little tube. The chemicals that come with the kit are added. The whole lot is shaken up and then allowed to settle. The colour of the tube's contents is then checked against the chart provided, giving a rough idea of the relative acidity or alkalinity of the soil. The pH of the soil in any garden can vary considerably within a small area. So it is important, and interesting, to take several samples.

Checking the pH level every few years can be revealing – and rewarding. We did this recently and found that the test confirmed what the worms had been telling us. Nineteen years of organic nourishment had improved the pH of the soil in my garden to an almost neutral state. There are many different kits available – some of them highly sophisticated. Buy one to suit your pocket – they all work.

❋ *Liming*

There's an old Yorkshire saying: 'Lime and lime without manure, makes both farm and farmer poor.' There's also an old 'rule' that you should never apply lime and manure at the same time. This second one is largely discounted now, but the warning in the first is still worth heeding – add lime when appropriate, but add it with caution. Lime may help 'sweeten' the soil, but it doesn't feed it in the way that manure does.

So-called 'garden lime' is hydrated lime, which has the disadvantage of being easily soluble. It can be washed out of the soil, especially a light soil, fairly quickly and requires regular replenishment (maybe as often as every two years). This is why most organic gardeners prefer the slower-working ground limestone, or dolomite, which lasts longer than hydrated lime; although you have to apply it in slightly greater amounts.

It's worth pointing out that calcified seaweed also raises the pH of soil, which is useful to remember as it contains valuable trace elements as well.

This isn't the only reason why lime improves soil. As I've said, it encourages worms. On clay soils lime has the additional merit of helping to improve soil structure. Lime encourages clay particles to clump together to form larger particles, which gradually leads to improved drainage. Lime will also help control the fungus that causes club-root.

According to Lawrence Hills, writing in *Fertility Without Fertilisers* (HDRA, 1975), ground limestone dressing should be applied to these soils in the following quantities:

Soil type	Dressing to change pH 4.5 to 5.5	Dressing to change pH 5.5 to 6.5
Sand and sandy loam	4 oz square yard	5 oz square yard
Loam	9 oz square yard	13 oz square yard
Clay loam	14 oz square yard	1 lb square yard

❋ DIGGING

Later in the book I'll be mentioning the advantages of growing vegetables in raised beds; all I'll say at this stage is that this is a system in which you garden without the need to dig over the plot every year.

This raises the interesting question of when and when not to dig, since digging for its own sake is not necessarily always to the soil's benefit. It depends very much on the sort of soil you have.

The whole point about digging is that it lets the gardener break up the soil's natural structure. This may be necessary if you want to start growing plants in a previously uncultivated plot. Digging also lets you add all sorts of soil-improving material: manure, compost, sharp sand, or whatever. Then there is the somewhat forbidding fact that digging is the only real way of dealing with poor drainage.

In the case where the soil doesn't need breaking up for any specific reason (with light, well-drained soils for instance), digging can do more harm than good. Worms and the hordes of microscopic creatures beavering away below the surface are doing far more good than the gardener with his or her spade. In fact the spade can undo a lot of their valuable work. Far better, in situations like this, to add organic material as a surface mulch, leaving the worms to take it underground in their own efficient time.

Though digging can be an effective way of getting rid of weeds, weed seeds can remain active in the soil for many years. Digging may bring them to the surface, exposing them to light and air and letting them burst forth with new-found energy. This can have something of a grim irony if you have spent several hours sweating and straining to get the last growth safely buried underground!

● *Double digging*

Before you reach for your spade, then, ask yourself whether or not digging is the best way of improving your soil (and spending a not inconsiderable amount of time and energy).

If you find yourself still reaching for your spade, you might consider the process known as double digging worth the extra effort involved. Breaking up a hard pan or heavy clay isn't a job you want to do more often than is necessary and double digging is an effective way of starting long-term soil improvement. (The same technique will help you establish the permanent raised beds that you won't ever have to dig again!)

Double digging is just that – you work the soil to two spades' depth; in single digging, you dig to just one spade's depth. The advantage that double digging brings is the chance to loosen the subsoil to a good depth and to add organic material to a good depth too.

Double digging is hard work, but as you're toiling away take comfort in knowing that you won't need to dig again for at least five years, if at all.

The important rule to remember is not to mix the topsoil with the subsoil. Try to keep the two separate.

You should start by digging your first strip (about two feed wide) to a spade's depth. Barrow all the topsoil from this to the end of the plot to fill your last trench.

Now loosen the soil below with a fork but don't turn it. Add manure or other organic material and work it in before taking the topsoil from the second strip and using this to fill the first trench, mixing in more organic material as you go.

Then you repeat the process, as far as possible keeping apart the two types of soil, working backwards until you reach the end and fill the last trench with topsoil brought from the first.

You may feel exhausted when you've finished,

but your drainage will have been immeasurably improved, any problem with it solved most likely, and there'll be lots of lovely, nutritious material for the worms and other soil 'improvers' to get to work on.

❋ DRAINAGE

How you tackle poor drainage depends on how serious the problem is, and how much time, effort and expense you are prepared to spend on improving it.

Some years ago I helped my sister in her new garden which had one corner where rainwater collected in wet weather; it became compacted in dry periods, and nothing she tried grew satisfactorily. I suppose a lot of hard work with the spade might have made things slightly better, but we decided to expend our energies more creatively. Instead of trying to grow plants in the waterlogged ground, we built a rockery and grew them well above it. Now she has a thriving colony of alpines which have turned a problem area into one of the most attractive aspects of her garden.

I doubt if you need me to tell you how to spot when your soil isn't draining. In the worst cases the only real solution may be installing a system of land drains to take away the excess water. But this is a job for skilled labour and not something to be undertaken lightly.

Less drastic action can improve less severe problems. Soil that becomes compacted, perhaps from being trodden down or walked across regularly (particularly in wet weather), can form a temporarily impervious layer, which digging will break up. Adding organic material and a bucket of sharp sand (not the smooth sand used by builders) to every square yard will go a long way to preventing this happening again.

Gardeners who save themselves the trouble of digging by using a mechanical rotovator sometimes find that turning the soil over to the same depth year after year can create what's known as a hard pan below the cultivated level. Digging through this will break it up too.

I've already mentioned that clay doesn't drain well and digging clay has a number of benefits, provided you choose the right time. You should never try to dig clay when it's wet. It's far too much work, for one thing. The wet clay will stick to everything (I enjoy getting mucky in the garden, but there is a limit). And you might make the situation worse by compacting the soil even more.

If you're lucky there may be a fine spell in late autumn, when the ground is dry enough to be workable, when you can dig it over to expose the large lumps to winter frosts that will break them up for you.

❀ FEEDING THE SOIL

Bulky organic material, like manure, does wonders in breaking up heavy soils. If that wasn't enough, it's a perfect raw material for the production of humus – that rich, brownish-black goo that every gardener craves. Humus helps retain moisture, produces plant foods of its own by encouraging microbes to get busy, helps plant roots to travel and darkens the soil, allowing it to warm quicker and retain heat longer than lighter soils.

You'll already appreciate my enthusiasm for manure! I practically kiss the farmers when they bring me a load and I'm sure the worms would too, given a chance – no wonder Ernest and Michael don't hang about on these occasions! I've uttered a few warnings in the previous chapter about checking the source of your manure, just to see whether any chemicals have found their way into it. Let me also repeat the warning that manure should be well rotted before you dig it in or spread it as a mulch around your plants. Pig and poultry manures have especially high concentrations of nutrients; if they are applied fresh, they can damage plants. However, they are splendid activators in compost heaps.

Most gardeners apply manure and compost in the spring or autumn, though you can make use of them at any time of the year. One barrowload will cover about four square yards. Compost can be added in great quantities if you wish to be generous.

Leafmould, which I also mentioned earlier, isn't high in nutrients but is an excellent source of bulky organic material – a sort of garden roughage, if you like. It helps structure the soil without providing plants with too much food. You might consider using leafmould as a substitute for peat, especially around acid-loving plants, now that the use of peat is being discouraged as it eventually dawns on us that it too is one of the earth's non-renewable resources. Spent coconut fibre (coir) is also available as a peat substitute. I have started to use this and feel very enthusiastic about it. It is clear, light, pleasant to handle and my seedlings have flourished. Maybe it dries out more quickly than peat-based composts, but it absorbs water more readily. I will most definitely continue using this material in the future.

When you're using a mulch (any sort of mulch), do make sure that you water the soil really well *before* spreading the mulching material. If you forget to water before mulching you have a problem, for one of the tasks a mulch does so efficiently is to retain moisture. It will also protect the surface of the soil from heavy rain, give the soil a lovely insulating blanket which keeps the warmth in once the sun has warmed it up, and slowly release plant foods. A mulch is one of the organic gardener's principal allies in dealing with weeds, but I'll deal with those in the next chapter. For the moment I want to concentrate on feeding the soil.

When I gardened at Timperley I bought bags of mushroom compost, which was wonderful stuff. Up in the Dales, the chalk contained in mushroom compost seemed a good way to reduce the acidity in the soil, apart from the beneficial effect I already knew it would have. So I ordered seventy bags. What I'd overlooked was that the mushroom compost that arrived at Timperley was dry. The load that came to my Dales home wasn't. It was saturated. There was nothing wrong with the mushroom compost *once* I'd moved it into the garden, sack by arm-wrenching sack. I just hope the plants appreciated my exertions. Believe me, dry mushroom compost has a lot to be said for it!

Anyone who can find a local supply of spent hops will find these a fairly cheap and good source of bulky organic matter. They contain some nutrients but their real benefit is in improving soil structure.

Similarly, gardeners who live near the coast will find a rich source of valuable trace elements and larger quantities of phosphate and potash in seaweed. You'll have to wash off the salt or leave the seaweed out in the rain for a couple of months before digging it in, but it rots quickly, so it won't need composting. (I've already mentioned that calcified seaweed is a useful supply of calcium to raise the pH in your soil, but it can be pricey.)

❂ *Fertilizers*

The plants we cultivate generally take more from the soil than they put back. Improving the soil by adding organic matter goes some way to helping redress this loss, as I've described, but it isn't necessarily the whole answer. Successful and sustainable growth is ensured by returning nutrients in the right amounts and the right rate, depending on the soil conditions and the plants that are being grown.

Nitrogen, potassium and phosphorus are the three major nutrients plants require, and these, along with trace elements, may sometimes need to be added by using fertilizers.

For the organic gardener the fertilizers in question are made from animal or plant waste, not artificially manufactured chemicals. I look on them as giving a fillip to my plants, a pick-me-up to encourage them when they're in need of a little extra nourishment, all the while maintaining their normal, wholesome diet of the various types of organic material I've already described.

At various times I've used the following organic fertilizers:

Seaweed meal This obviously has all the properties of seaweed mentioned above. I always use this (or bonemeal) when I'm planting any shrub. They both release their nutrients slowly.

SM3 Seaweed feed I use this as a foliar spray (on the leaves) to improve plant health and growth.

*Blood, fish and bone Blood, fish and bone acts faster than some of the others on the list. It's a good all-round fertilizer. You can use it on the lawn in the spring.

Comfrey liquid and nettle liquid Wonderful stuff which is easy to make. In fact, they are both so good they have a section all to themselves in the next chapter.

*Hoof and horn Rich in nitrogen, it releases its nutrients slowly. I use it in spring as a dressing around the base of plants that are pruned quite heavily, like raspberries. Jo likes using it on lawns.

*Dried blood Like hoof and horn, it has a high nitrogen content, though unlike hoof and horn it releases this quite quickly. It's useful on vegetables and lawns.

Burnt seashells I've read recently that these are very good for lime-loving plants – another idea for people with easy access to the coast.

*These fertilisers are a matter of choice and since the BSE crisis I have avoided them.

● *Green manures*

Green manures are some of the cheapest and easiest ways of improving the soil. Don't be misled by the name. We're not talking about heaps of unpleasant smelling, bilious muck. Green manures

are plants, such as buckwheat, fenugreek and
Hungarian rye, specifically grown to produce
bulky organic material, usually on spare ground,
that can be dug in whenever the plot is not needed
to grow something else.

I must be honest and say that I'm not terribly
good at taking full advantage of green manures,
because invariably I seem to miss the boat with the
short growing season I have at home. But I'm very
much in favour of using them. Rather than just
leaving a patch of soil empty through the winter
(or at any other time of the year, for that matter), it
makes such good sense to grow something quick
and easy which will put goodness back into the
soil.

Green manures have a number of advantages
provided they are dug in while they are still imma-
ture, before flowering. Not the least of their benefits is that they return the plant foods that they
absorbed while growing, adding humus as a
bonus.

One of the most useful things a green manure
does is to protect the soil, particularly from heavy
rain. This makes them very useful in winter. The
leaves on green manure crops shelter the soil surface from the constant pounding of raindrops, and
this stops a hard crust forming on the surface. The
plants draw up soil nutrients while they're growing, saving these from being washed away by the
same heavy rain. And the thick foliage discourages
weeds.

Worms and micro-organisms are happiest
where plants are growing, so a green manure will
keep them in a plot between one crop cultivation
and the next.

Certain green manures belonging to the pea

family add nitrogen to the soil as they decompose. Others have long roots that penetrate deep into the subsoil drawing up nutrients seldom reached by other plants. So one way and another every garden can benefit from their use.

They're certainly not difficult to grow. Depending on their size, green manure seeds can be broadcast or sown in a narrow furrow known as a drill. Green manures left in the ground during the winter can be dug in the following spring before they flower, to fertilize the soil. Those planted in the growing season will be ready to dig in between a month and two months after sowing, though you can dig them in sooner if you want to make use of the plot for another crop.

Mustard is traditionally a popular green manure, producing an abundance of green leaves in only a few weeks when it's sown in summer. The one drawback with mustard is that it is prone to clubroot, prolonging the presence of that particular garden blight if your soil already suffers from it.

The ones I've mentioned are among the most commonly cultivated green manures, and a seed catalogue from the Henry Doubleday Research Association or Chase Organics will probably mention others that might suit your particular circumstances. I've tried buckwheat, which grows quickly when it's sown in the summer. The bees and hoverflies are attracted by it, which is another commendation as far as I'm concerned.

I bought some cereal rye (not to be confused with perennial rye grass) last year but events overtook me and I missed the chance to plant it. I've resolved to make sure that I do get round to it this year, because I like the idea of keeping the ground active all the time and not leaving it empty.

Like so many aspects of organic gardening, there just seems to be something right and wholesome about putting back into the soil the things that are natural to it.

For a gardener, that surely has to be the best form of husbandry.

5 Taming and Tackling Weeds

> ...'tis an unweeded garden
> That grows to seed.'
>
> William Shakespeare
> *Hamlet*

I don't know how much Shakespeare really knew about gardening, but this memorable line from *Hamlet* strikes a chord, if not a knell of foreboding, with everyone who cares about keeping a garden looking at its best. The trouble with weeding is that it's easy to get so carried away that you end up zealously clearing the garden of plants that are actually serving a very useful purpose. Here's Shakespeare again, this time writing in *Richard II*, to put the words into so many gardeners' mouths:

> ... I will go root away,
> The noisome weeds, that without profit suck
> The soil's fertility from wholesome flowers.

From following the principles of organic gardening I can now confidently say that I incline towards Ralph Waldo Emerson's opinion that a weed is 'a plant whose virtues have not been discovered'. There is a value in the lowly plants which can so easily be overlooked. Comfrey and stinging nettles, for instance, are two of my favourites and I'll be extolling their virtues shortly.

For the time being let me concentrate on ways I've tried to tackle the weeds that I really don't want growing where nature has thought to place them.

For my first three years in the Dales the weeding was frantic. The garden had just been meadowland, so everything that grows happily in a pasture was well rooted there. Add to that the fact that large areas of soil were bare after my initial planting, before the plants had the chance to become established, the weeds went wild – they literally had a field day!

At the time the value of mulching couldn't really have dawned on me. Together, the moss, the stones and the weeds kept me hard at it. I was lucky in having help with cutting the grass and trimming the edges, but even so, just keeping the garden looking tidy seemed like a never-ending job. It was my equivalent of painting the Forth Bridge. Not that I mind weeding; in reasonable spurts I love it. It gives one thinking time and brings one in close contact with growing things. But it was the relentless struggle to keep pace with the weeds until the plants became established that I found so demanding. I think if I hadn't known from my previous garden that organic methods win through in the end, if you persevere, the temptation to reach for a weed-killing spray might have been quite hard to resist. Backed by this confidence and the help I had I stuck to my guns, my plants gradually crowded out the weeds and boy, was I glad!

❋ CLEARING NEGLECTED GARDENS AND ROUGH GROUND

For anyone starting a garden from scratch, or trying to rehabilitate one that has been allowed to return a little too enthusiastically to nature, the most satisfactory way of dealing with perennial weeds, if you can bear it, is to put down a thick light-excluding mulch. Old carpets and cardboard are ideal for this and they're also very cheap, or even free. You can use thick layers of newspapers too. Thick black plastic is a possibility; so is old lino. All of them will block out light and without light plants will die.

The trouble is that these mulches really need to be left in place for a year to stifle perennial weeds properly, and none of them are the most attractive things to have lying in your garden for twelve months. You could cover them with a layer of soil to improve their appearance, but you should reckon on that part of the garden not looking its best for a year. It's a case of the end justifying the means.

I have to admit that my first attempt at using newspaper wasn't an unqualified success. The one thing we have no shortage of in the Dales is stones. I also had a pile of old newspapers in the house at the time when I thought I should do something about the weeds growing round my soft fruit: some raspberry canes, a gooseberry bush and a blackcurrant bush. They were growing in part of the garden hidden from the house, so trying the newspapers, held down by stones, as a weed-killing mulch seemed a sound organic idea.

But when I came home from a week away there wasn't a newspaper to be seen in its rightful place! It had been a particularly windy few days and there was newspaper all over the garden. All through the weekend I kept finding it blown into obscure corners or lifted tantalizingly just out of my reach. That taught me the need of using a really thick mulch, well held down.

I suppose I could have put soil over the top, because eventually newspapers would have rotted down. Carpet will rot down too, given time. But carpet is easier to control, provided a hurricane doesn't pay you a visit. Though it's still a good idea to peg it down or hold it down with weights.

● *Pathways*

Keeping pathways in the vegetable garden free of weeds can be another very time-consuming occupation. If you put a heavy-weight mulch under the surface layer it will block out the light from any weeds lurking underneath and should save a bit of work.

I've put down old carpet, or thick plastic bags like the ones that garden materials such as compost come in. My local farmer also gives me thick bags that some of his materials are delivered in.

As for the surface of the path, I use wood shavings, wood chippings, and shredded woody garden waste. I've also put down some conifer clippings which look very nice. The only danger with these is that some people might find them a little bit slippery when they're wet. (As a matter of interest, I've recently read that conifer cuttings can be used to protect plants during the winter. You just stick them in around the plant and bend them over to provide a little wall of protection from frost.)

● *Mulches to suppress weeds*

Thick, chunky forest bark (as opposed to composted forest bark) is useful for keeping weeds under control. You need a layer three inches thick to do the job properly.

Grass cuttings will stifle weeds too, and are useful provided that they don't contain weed seeds themselves. You can use grass cuttings between plants, though you must keep them away from plant stems. Grass cuttings will heat up as they rot down and may harm them.

Hay and straw will stifle weeds too, but if a garden is windy they can be more of a problem than they're worth, blowing everywhere and making the place look untidy. Both also carry the risk of harbouring weed seeds.

Before applying any of these mulches, it's terribly important to water the soil well beforehand.

❊ *Mulches to suppress weeds and improve the soil*

I've already described my first experience with mushroom compost – marvellous when it's dry!

At first I spread this too thinly to be an effective mulch against weeds. Even so, those weeds that did grow through were easily deal with and of course the mushroom compost helped nourish the soil at the same time. It can be expensive, as I've said, and looking around you can often find cheaper organic mulches that will look just as attractive.

I suspect that, like a lot of gardeners, I had never been used to spending a lot of money on my garden. So starting to buy things like the more costly mulches was quite a big step. Mind you, it became easier once I stopped smoking! That was fifteen years ago, and the money that I'd previously spent on cigarettes was now free to be spent on the garden. I didn't even feel extravagant – just very grateful to a hypnotist. One of my first expensive purchases under this new regime was composted forest bark, which looks so lovely. It smells wonderful too – a bit like a brewery I suppose, rich and heady. The plants look superb set against it, and in my book it's worth every penny.

To suppress weeds the bark should really be at least three inches deep and ideally you should replenish it each spring. Bark is a good soil conditioner, but it will deplete the nitrogen in the soil as it decomposes if it is dug in. Leave it to the worms to do the job very gradually, and then you will enjoy its benefits as a mulch first and as a soil conditioner later.

Leafmould, made at home as I've described earlier, will suppress weeds and improve the soil. So will homemade compost. If you have a ready source of seaweed, that's supposed to be good too. And so are chopped comfrey *and* chopped nettles. Provided you don't get the seed heads or roots in your chopped nettles, there's a nice irony about using them to control weeds and improve the soil at the same time; though as I'll soon be explaining, nettles are full of useful properties for anyone willing to look beyond their sting.

Not all nettles in the garden are going to be wanted and it is generally accepted that nettles (in fact most weeds) will eventually give up the struggle if they are constantly and remorselessly cut to the ground.

The timing of cutting can sometimes play a part in its success, or otherwise. There's a saying about thistles:

> Cut in June – Cut too soon
> Cut in July – Sure to die.

So provided the thistles haven't seeded, leave cutting them back until June has passed.

Apparently a teaspoonful of salt in the middle of a dandelion plant will finish that off in time. I can't say that I have great faith in this, but some gardeners find it successful. You have to watch that you don't pollute your garden with too much salt, of course.

If this wasn't a problem I'd cover my garden with salt just to be rid of the slugs, which brings me to the major problem of using mulches. They can provide wonderful hidey holes and shelter for my *bêtes noires*, or orange or brown, or whatever colour the slugs choose to come in. I'll be mentioning various slug traps and slug-preventing ploys I've tried later, but seedlings in particular are at risk from slug damage if slug-sheltering mulches are close by.

❁   *Hand-weeding and hoeing*

I feel I can speak with some experience of hand-weeding after my early years in the Dales. If you're dealing with weeds that send down deep tap roots, careful hand-weeding which removes a large part, if not all, of the root, is the only certain way of removing the weed – the only certain organic way, that is – apart perhaps from a flame thrower.

Hand-weeding also allows the gardener to exercise the greatest degree of care if weeds have to be removed from borders or beds where plants are tightly packed.

Hoeing is an ideal method of tackling annual weeds where you have more space to work. It's a marvellous way of ploughing back the plants together with the nutrients they have taken from the soil.

● *Tagetes minuta*

Since a lot of gardens suffer the unwelcome attention of couch grass, ground elder and horse-tail, it's worth mentioning that the marigold *Tagetes minuta* is said to be a weedkiller par excellence. The secretions and excretions from its roots are reputed to be capable of killing all three. I wish I'd known this when I gardened at Altrincham and suffered from the twenty-foot-high privet hedge festooned in convolvulus.

Wireworms, eelworms and millipedes are said to be destroyed by this marigold too. Seeds of *Tagetes minuta* are not easy to find, but some of its properties are attributed to *Tagetes erecta* as well. This is the African marigold, not a flower I have liked in the past – always preferring the simple pot marigolds, the calendulas. Henceforth *Tagetes erecta* and *Tagetes patula*, the French marigold, will be welcome in my garden.

● THE VALUE OF THE LOWLY PLANTS

After talking at some length about ways of getting rid of plants, let me now dwell on some of the reasons why we should pause for a moment to consider what benefit a plant might be bringing to the garden, before we uproot it. I'd like to concentrate in particular on comfrey and stinging nettles, which until recently have been two of our least appreciated and most abundant plants.

Nettles and comfrey will add carbon and nitrogen to the soil in a balance similar to farmyard manure. Nettles also provide iron, and comfrey is high in calcium, potassium and phosphorus. Both are invaluable in the organic garden – particularly as contributors to and activators of the compost heap. They really deserve a chapter all of their own for they bring so much fertility into the soil. Dandelions, too, are rich in iron. Their deep roots – haven't we all raged against them? – restore calcium to the topsoil, copper too, and the plant provides many other nutrients which are beneficial if composted. I would avoid putting the roots or seeded flower-heads on the compost heap but the leaves and flowers are as gold.

These wonder herbs are not only great gardeners, but for more than 2,000 years they have been valued for their medicinal properties. In addition, the nettle has been used as a vegetable and the dandelion as a delicious salad ingredient. Nor does praise stop there. I have made wines from them – very acceptable wines, with the added appeasement to my conscience that they are *really* good for one!

So never despise a humble weed – they are giants of scientific complexity – there are many books to be found on herbs, weeds, their identification and uses. Beware, once you start to read about them, you won't want to stop – and the gardening can't be left undone!

❀ Comfrey

There are many species of comfrey, part of a huge family of plants, *Boraginaceae*, which includes the beautiful herb borage, whose gorgeously blue, starry flowers look so pretty when frozen in ice cubes and added to summer drinks and salads.

The best plant for gardens is the Russian

comfrey (*Symphytum* × *uplandicum*). This is not easy to grow from seed, so it is advisable to plant a piece of root, which is usually obtainable from the HDRA at Ryton Gardens and is known as Bocking 14; it was so named at the original test ground in Essex.

Henry Doubleday (1813–1902) originally imported Russian comfrey into England from the royal palace in St Petersburg, hoping to use it commercially. He ran a factory which produced gum for postage stamps and, finding problems in obtaining gum arabic from Egypt, he sought an alternative. He had been impressed by an analysis of comfrey but found the proteins in the plants, which had been described as mucilaginous, were of no use to him in his production process.

They may not have been useful to stamp-licking Victorians, but, thanks to Henry Doubleday's continued interest and research into the plant, we now know the huge benefits which this very special plant can give to any garden.

Among vegetables, only the soya bean has a higher percentage of protein. Comfrey contains vitamins and minerals comparable to spinach, and it can extract the vitamin B12 from the soil. Henry Doubleday believed so strongly in the merits of comfrey that he dreamed of its large-scale production becoming the answer to world famine. Sadly this did not happen in his lifetime and he died a poor man, who, as a Quaker smallholder, had not sought to make profit from his 'wonder herb'. Fortunately his banner was carried aloft by the late Lawrence D. Hills, founder and president of the HDRA, and now at Ryton Gardens visitors can see comfrey being grown and used in many different ways.

Do try to find space in the garden for some comfrey. Even one plant will repay the square yard you give to it by providing you with nine or ten pounds of organic matter each season. Larger gardens, smallholdings and farms can expect to crop something in the region of fifty tons per acre – no mean harvest from a 'common weed'. Once you have established your plants of Russian comfrey you can expect up to twenty years' cropping from them. Plants can be increased if all leaves are cut to soil level, a spade used to split up the plant, and new plants grown from small sections of root, providing each piece has a growing tip. Plant the new sections in ordinary soil which is free of perennial weeds.

Russian comfrey requires no special conditions. It is almost entirely pest-free and disease-free. If, as occasionally might happen, the plant is attacked by rust, the only thing to do is to get rid of it, but this is not a likely problem.

The most important role of comfrey in my garden is its use as a compost plant. I manage to get three cuts of leaves in a season – the new spring leaves and the middle-sized ones for drying, and the whopping big, wonderful, hairy, monster-sized leaves for the compost heap, vegetable trenches, or for making comfrey liquid plant food. If I kept chickens, or indeed any livestock, I would try to grow a bed of comfrey especially for them as a super-tonic source of food.

Apart from adding its impressive array of minerals, vitamins and proteins to the layers in the compost heap, its assistance in breaking down vegetation in the heap is invaluable. Used alone or together with nettles it beats all other compost activators. I have room for only two plants but can find others growing wild in the lanes nearby and so harvest those leaves too. The plants are so generous in their growth that they don't look denuded for very long, and no damage has been done to the countryside.

It is best to cut the leaves (wear gloves always as there are fine prickly hairs on the undersides which penetrate the skin like needles) and allow them to wilt for a day or so before adding them to the compost heap. There is not enough fibre to make a heap of comfrey alone, so make sure it is well mixed with other materials.

Comfrey can be chopped and used as a mulch with grass cuttings in equal proportions – again, allow the comfrey to wilt for a day before chopping and using. It will help to conserve moisture in the soil and feed greedy plants at the same time. Remember to be careful not to let the mulch touch the stems of plants you are mulching and use it one to two inches deep.

I always lay comfrey in the potato trenches, plant the potatoes on a good handful of homemade compost, tell the potatoes that I've done my best for them – the rest is up to them – and leave them to it. So far crops have always been good. I think the comfrey keeps them healthy. Once again the only villains have been slugs. Tomatoes and beans also benefit greatly by being raised on comfrey-enriched beds.

An excellent foliar feed and liquid manure is made by packing a container with chopped comfrey leaves, filling it with water, leaving it for three weeks or more, syphoning off the dark (very smelly) liquid and using it diluted 10 to 20 parts of water to one of comfrey liquid. Nettles can be used in the same way, or mixed with comfrey, to provide a free, rich source of nutrition to the garden – wholly organic and unbeatable.

As comfrey is such a special food for our gardens, so it is for animals on the farm or in our houses. Indeed, I have read that at one time it was grown in large quantities for feeding animals at Whipsnade Zoo, and was top favourite with the hippopotamus, who was clearly 'no ignoramus' and must have known full well what he was about! I hope very much they're still growing comfrey at Whipsnade. The benefits to livestock are said to be many when it is used to treat digestive problems and to promote good health and vigour in all creatures, as well as providing an easily digested and bounteous fodder.

The old names for comfrey like 'knitbone' and 'boneset' were not lightly given, and much has been written about this plant's exceptional contributions in the field of herbal medicine.

G.J. Binding's book *About Comfrey – the forgotten herb* (1974) quotes Pliny the Elder, writing in the first century BC, who said of comfrey:

> The roots be so glutinative that they will solder or glew together meat that is chopt in pieces, seething in a pot and make it into one lump, the same bruised and lay'd in the manner of a plaster doth heale all flesh and green wounds.

In the past, comfrey has been used as a cough cure, for sinus problems, for the healing of broken bones, sprains, bruises, burns, fractures, liver problems, skin complaints, arthritis, rheumatism and muscular strain or stiffness. And here I come to a dilemma. Should I go on to extol what I believe to be the considerable medicinal virtues of comfrey which I and many others have experienced – or should I draw a discreet veil over the subject? I think I will mention some other aspects.

These are the facts as I understand them. At present comfrey has not been subjected to the rigorous scientific tests which might, or might not, support the beneficial anecdotal evidence amassed by herbalists over many centuries. As a result, comfrey products are under some question; in Switzerland and Germany their use has already been banned. Until funds have been made available to undertake the required scientific tests the availability of comfrey products hangs in the balance. As far as I and my garden are concerned I feel very comforted to know that I have a good supply of leaves ready to hand.

I think I should repeat my earlier caution that it is always advisable to consult your doctor or health adviser and inform them if you are using a herbal remedy, and certainly for anything long-lasting, it is essential to seek proper professional help.

❂   *Stinging nettles*

I must have been about five years old, living in the country and visiting a friend's father's farm. At the side of the lane there was an old cart, long since abandoned, over which I decided to scramble. Reaching the furthest edge, which was tipped high in the air I stretched tall, shouting 'I'm the King of the Castle' and fell backwards into a huge bed of stinging nettles. I was marooned. My sister and friend couldn't reach me. I was in shock, on fire, my bare hands, arms and legs and face covered in nettle stings. Somehow I found the courage to stand and push through these monstrous, torturing plants and was taken, bawling loudly to my mother and the farmer's wife, who immediately covered my painful limbs with dock leaves. I can't remember how long it took for the cooling effects of the dock to be effective, but I know it worked and I well remember being given a big glass of rich, warm milk – straight from the cow – as a reward for being brave. Brave? I'd screamed the place down! Though once more the old adage had been proved right,

> When bairn's fingers nettles find,
> See old red Dock is close behind.

I've read that Roman soldiers brought the seed of the Roman nettle with them, so that they could be sure of a ready supply to rub on their arms and legs when the bitter cold of the British climate made them stiff and numb. I think I'd rather have endured the cold, but each to his own.

It must be the sting of the nettle which has blinded most of us to the plant's wonderful properties in the garden, herbal medicine cabinet and even the kitchen.

I've already mentioned the invaluable part nettles play in a compost heap. Even left to rot down on their own, nettles produce rich dark humus which would be the envy of most gardeners.

The experience of countless gardeners shows that nettles, far from depleting soil nutrients from cultivated plants growing nearby, positively enhance their growth and welfare. This is particularly true in the case of soft fruits like raspberries, goose-berries, blackcurrants and redcurrants.

Rich in most of the elements that we require, nettles can similarly enhance human well-being. The vitamin C in nettles will help keep colds at bay, while nettle teas will sooth sore throats.

Flogging with nettles used to be considered a remedy for rheumatism and in gentler forms of herbal medicine nettles are prescribed for the relief of bronchitis, asthma and gout.

Nettles lose their sting when heated, which makes the idea of eating them more palatable than it may first sound. Cooked with leeks, broccoli and rice, nettles were widely and enthusiastically eaten in earlier times. Samuel Pepys tucked into some nettle porridge in February 1661 and noted in his diary that it was 'very good'.

His porridge, or pudding, would probably have been similar to this recipe.

Ingredients
1 gallon of young nettle tops (picked with gloved hand!)
2 leeks or onions
2 heads of broccoli (a small cabbage, or brussels sprouts can be used instead)
1/2lb of rice

Method
Clean and wash the nettles and vegetables. Chop the vegetables and mix them with the nettles. Add this mixture to the rice and place in a muslin bag. Tie this tightly and boil it in salted water until the vegetables are cooked to your liking. Serve with gravy or butter; there should be enough for five or six people.

At one time, nettles were used to produce a cloth, not unlike linen. The Scottish poet, Thomas Campbell (1777–1844), commented critically on the scant attention paid to the nettle south of the border and informed his readers:

> In Scotland, I have eaten nettles, I have slept in nettle sheets, and I have dined off a nettle table-cloth. The young and tender nettle is an excellent potherb. The stalks of the old nettle are as good as flax for making cloth. I have heard my mother say that she thought nettle cloth more durable than any other species of linen.

As recently as the First World War, nettle fibre was an important textile in Germany, used in the weaving of a considerable amount of army clothing, from shirts to gas masks.

In France nettles were once collected to be made into paper.

But before straying too far from organic gardening, let me make the simple plea that you preserve at least a small clump of nettles for the benefit of butterflies. Some species rely entirely on nettles for their food.

If a weed ever had value beyond one's expectations it has to be the nettle, a sentiment aptly summed up in the couplet,

> Where the hurt shall bring you woe,
> God made the healing herb to grow.

❀ Dandelion

In the garden, dandelions have less to offer than comfrey and stinging nettles. Their long tap roots will draw up nutrients from depths seldom reached by many other plants, but set against this is the ethylene gas which they exhale and which can hamper the growth of surrounding plants. It's on the compost heap or converted into a foliar feed that they really commend themselves to the organic gardener. And if the gardener happens to have a penchant for salads, the dandelion will certainly win favour.

Medicinally, dandelions have been used for centuries to clear up skin infections, to deal with liver complaints and kidney disorders.

Today I think the dandelion wins most friends in the kitchen. It's said to be high in vitamins A and C. Mixed with other salad vegetables, tender young dandelion leaves give a delicious piquant flavour.

The same leaves can be cooked slowly with butter to provide a tasty table vegetable, served with a squeeze of lemon.

Dandelions go particularly well with spinach, either cooked, or as a salad as given here.

Ingredients
1 pint of loosely-packed young dandelion leaves
1 pint of loosely-packed young spinach leaves
A few dandelion buds
2 or 3 rashers of smoked bacon
Oil and vinegar

Method
Wash and dry the salad leaves. Grill or fry the bacon until crisp. If frying, throw the buds into the bacon fat. Drain the buds and bacon on paper towels. Crush bacon into small pieces and add to the leaves in the salad bowl. Add dressing and serve.

While dandelion coffee (made from the roots) may not quite be up to serving after dinner, it makes a gentle, soothing bedtime drink which tastes weaker than coffee, but doesn't contain the caffeine that could have you awake and buzzing half the night.

All things considered, weeds have much to commend them if they're looked at beyond the narrow confines of garden order. Audrey Wynne Hatfield's book *How to Enjoy Your Weeds* (1969) will tell you about lots more. But do heed my earlier warning – once you start reading, you won't want to put the book down and then the weeds really will present you with a challenge!

6 Coping with Pests and Diseases

'...slugs leave their lair –
The bees are stirring – birds are on the wing –'

Samuel Taylor Coleridge
'Work Without Hope'

If there's one thing guaranteed to test an organic gardener's resolve, it's coming face to face with the damage wrought by pests and disease.

I say 'one thing', but here lies the difficulty. These tribulations seldom come singly. Roses can be infested with greenfly, be covered with black spot and mildew and show signs of rust all at the same time. And that's just one example. In the vegetable garden the slugs can be gorging themselves fit to bust, birds will be carrying out round-the-clock sorties on the soft fruit, while below ground all manner of bugs and spores will be attacking anything that grows. Meanwhile, garden centre shelves will be generously stocked with a battery of chemical 'solutions' that will rid you of the problem as if by magic.

I have a little poem that I like to recall at times like this. I wrote it years ago for my children when they were young, and long before I even had an inkling of what organic gardening stood for; it must have been a portent of times to come.

At the bottom of our garden,
Beneath a great big stone,
A lot of wriggly woodlice live –

They'd called that place their home.
But Daddy came along today
And with a puff and squirt
Of something deadly – killed the lot
Now all that's left is dirt.

I quoted that when I was very kindly asked to
open the HDRA gardens at Ryton. Organic gardening certainly teaches you (and requires you) to take
a more tolerant attitude to the damage that pests
and disease can cause. Having said that, it also
teaches you lots of ways in which you can drasti-
cally reduce the damage to the point where you
can live comfortably with the other denizens of the
garden and still enjoy masses of your own fruit
and vegetables, not to mention your flowers – with
the reassuring knowledge that none of them have
lingering chemical residues.

Things certainly don't happen overnight with
organic gardening. It may take a few years to nurture the soil into good condition, but patience is
rewarded; as the soil becomes healthier, so do the
plants.

Pests and disease also seem to be less of a
problem, which puzzled me for some time. I can
understand why healthy plants resist disease, but I
found it hard to believe that they would also resist
pests. Surely any marauding aphid would be happier to munch on an organically cultivated leaf
rather than a chemically saturated one. If I were a
hungry caterpillar, I know where I'd want to be
dining.

Fortunately I am wrong. Plants grown in
organic soil are that bit tougher and able to resist
damage from aphids who just love the softer,
sappier growth which is the hallmark of artificially

fed plants. Cabbage white caterpillars and aphids are also attracted to plants which are higher in nitrate, so organic gardeners can score points here too.

This does seem to be the case in my own garden, where the plants seem strong enough on the whole to withstand the sudden infestation of unwanted pests.

We should tolerate some damage – a few holes in a cabbage leaf won't hurt, and eating it will be much more beneficial than eating one which has been drenched with chemicals. Understanding and striving for natural balance in the garden counts for a great deal in successful organic gardening.

I sing a lot in the garden, though where that fits into the scheme of natural balance is not for me to say! Fortunately for my neighbours they are some distance away and I don't sing very loudly. My plants don't complain and my gardener finds it unusual but quite amusing and seems to accept that actresses can be a bit eccentric.

I do talk to the inhabitants of my garden, be they animals, bird, insect or plant life. We know that domestic animals respond to our efforts to communicate with them, so it seems arrogant on our part to assume that other creatures, other forms of life for that matter, don't have sensitivity too. I think we just haven't yet found the key to communicate with them, but I am sure our feelings of care and goodwill are in some way transmitted and create a happy, well-loved atmosphere in the garden, as they would in the home, or anywhere else we may be. That is not to say everything is always sweetness and light; a hydrangea which didn't flower for three years was given regular dressing-downs and finally an ultimatum that it would be forcibly removed if no flowers appeared the next year. Shamefaced and half-hearted, it managed just a few glorious heads last year – so it has won a reprieve and this year has flowers galore.

Then there was the occasion, two years ago, when I had a visitation from some wild bees. They decided to become resident. Suddenly there was tremendous activity in the wall of my cottage, which is a renovated barn. The builders had used stone from the roof inside a niche built into the wall. The bees were flying in and out through a hole in the roofing stone which had been left by the removal of a nail. It was obviously not a good idea to have this particular commotion going on just when one wanted to collapse into a deck chair on a summer evening, glass in hand, with the day's work done.

I enquired how I was to remove them, or persuade them to leave. The prognosis wasn't good. They would have to be smoked out. Now, I like bees, knowing what terrific work they do in the garden, but they couldn't live in the house – so another ultimatum had to be issued. I remembered reading somewhere that bee-keepers told their bees of any happenings in the family, so I had a good heart-to-heart and asked them very politely if they would kindly leave the premises, as, much as I appreciated all they did for me in the garden, they would have to seek other accommodation or be forcibly evicted the next week.

By the time the ultimatum expired, incredibly, there were only two or three bees left. I think they'd stayed behind to tidy up and say 'goodbye' – I thanked them. They had saved me from a decision I was dreading having to put into operation.

A colleague and friend, Geoff Hinsliff, moved his home and family to Manchester from Essex where he had kept bees. He decided that a town house wasn't the place for his hobby, but kept one of his hives to be a decorative element in his new garden. Well, he may have given up on bees, but they hadn't given up on him and within a few weeks a swarm had taken up residence in his empty hive. They must have known a good bee-keeper when they saw one.

I have since tried talking to slugs and have asked them to leave my garden, please. They are either deaf or defiant – they are certainly insatiably greedy and still there.

I've learnt that the first rule in dealing with slugs or another pest or plant disease is to tackle the problem early, and this calls for vigilance and a beady eye. If you train yourself to be really observant, to look closely at plants, you'll be surprised how quickly you can start to notice when they're off colour or under threat. Problems noticed early can be dealt with early. At the same time, looking closely at plants definitely develops an affinity with the plant you're growing and an increasing wonderment and awe at the variety and beauty of the natural world.

The message has to be don't look at your *garden*, look at each *plant* – specifically. It takes more of your time, but the reward is incalculable. You will be able to appreciate the form, individuality, colour, scent, precision, health and beauty of each miracle of nature.

This intimate awareness will then lead you on to a deeper concern for its welfare and you will begin to notice very early on any changes which may take place in its well-being and be able to take immediate steps to control the attacking pest or disease.

I was so appalled to see my beautiful Aloha rose stems covered in early greenfly one year that, for the first time, I was able to strip them off with my bare fingers – a modest claim, you may feel, but I am squeamish about killing anything and I really felt I could call myself a gardener once I had overcome my distaste.

Variety in your planting will help a great deal as well – so will intermingling your plants as much as possible. I'll be dealing with companion planting in greater detail later, but it's worth mentioning here that some plants can be particularly helpful in promoting the health and combating some types of disease in certain others, if they are planted close together.

If variety in your garden can mirror, even to a tiny extent, the variety of plants that grow naturally you'll be going some way to creating a harmonious environment with all the natural benefits that stem from it. Though I'm no mathematician this can be summed up in a neat equation:

$$\left.\begin{array}{l}\text{Plants attract insects as food} \\ \text{Insects attract predators as food}\end{array}\right\} = \text{Balance}$$

Let me give a specific example of this symbiosis at work in my own garden. As I've indicated, it's taken me several years to get to the point where I can 'squidge' greenfly with my fingers. It's not pleasant, but I steel myself and still wear gloves to do it, when I can.

Aphids usually arrive in my garden before the ladybirds and hoverflies which feed on them. But as soon as the Limnanthes (poached egg plant) is in flower I can relax. The hoverflies adore these for their nectar and pollen and as a result visit the garden and lay their eggs near a good supply of food (aphids) and I leave the rest to them. Ladybirds can be brought home in a matchbox from walks and introduced into the garden (if one feels 'understocked'), and I think they are now available commercially in this country.

This brings to mind a story told to me by a make-up artist I know who's also a keen gardener. For reasons that she didn't go into, or I've forgotten, she found herself asked to supply her doctor with a urine sample collected over several days one hot summer a year or two ago. Although I've no evidence to support this supposition, I've a pretty shrewd idea that the technology devised for collecting urine samples was dreamt up by a man, for whom the process would no doubt have seemed straightforward enough. For the female of the species, this is not necessarily so. In my friend's case it certainly wasn't.

Receiving a call of nature while in the thick of battling with the aphids attacking her roses, she remembered the need to collect her sample, which under the circumstances was obtained with haste and not inconsiderable inconvenience.

When the results came through a few days later, the nurse who saw her passed on the good news that whatever the tests had been looking for, they had proved negative. 'Mind you,' the nurse added, 'we'll have to give you something to sort out your other problem. That's a very nasty attack of greenfly you've got. Would you like to see a doctor or an entomologist?'

My gardening friends' experiences seem often to be inextricably linked with humour and basic human need. Joan, my bosom pal in Bristol, found herself locked out of her house in bad weather and decided to spend the time tidying the garden shed until a member of the family came home to let her in.

One hour dragged into two during which time the wind blew the shed door shut, the catch engaged and she was trapped inside in dire need of the loo. She's a resourceful lady and took action – needs must when the devil drives. The only receptacle available was a watering can with a sloping top opening, over which was a central handle. Shall I go on? Suffice to say that with a great deal of difficulty the task was accomplished – made not a jot easier by the fact that she found it hilariously funny and laughed a lot. She now makes sure that her garden equipment always includes the odd bucket or two, and never stops being grateful that she's been a yoga enthusiast for years.

Another way of protecting your plants against disease in particular is the very choice of the plants themselves. The HDRA and other suppliers of organic seeds take a great deal of care in developing plant strains that can resist some of the most prevalent diseases that have attacked similar varieties in the past. Planting these in your own garden helps reduce problems at the outset.

In the same way it's important to watch for problems that can be innocently imported from other gardens. This isn't always easy, especially when friends and neighbours generously offer cuttings or plants. No garden soil can be guaranteed disease free, so there's bound to be a risk attached to accepting donations like this, but I am always prepared to overlook that for the pleasure of remembering friends as I enjoy their gifts in my garden.

Crop rotation, which I'll also be covering in greater detail later (in chapter 7, Fruit and Vegetable Growing), is another intelligent way of minimizing the potential damage soil-borne disease can cause. I practise a four-year rotation in my vegetable garden, so that no groups of vegetables are in the same soil more often than one year in four. With a system like this, diseases have less chance to become well established and some crops will leave behind elements that can significantly benefit the ones that follow them. Once again the gardener enlists nature to combat natural threats in a totally natural way.

Keeping the garden tidy is another simple but amazingly effective preventive measure. I don't mean keeping it obsessively tidy, but making sure that fallen leaves, diseased with mildew or blackspot for example, are cleared away to prevent reinfection the following year. Plant debris can provide marvellous hiding places for all manner of garden pests. Disease-free material can go straight on to the compost heap and anything that is diseased can either be taken off to the rubbish dump or rapidly burned in a quick-blazing bonfire.

All of these are simple, practical measures any gardener can take to reduce problems. But they won't eradicate them altogether. In an organic garden nothing will – but the organic gardener wouldn't want it to, either. The organic gardener seeks balance. As far as the kitchen goes, for instance, we tolerate a slightly nibbled apple or cabbage because of the certain knowledge that the taste, texture and structure are totally chemical-free.

The next step in dealing with pests, at any rate, is to enlist the help of their natural predators by providing a safe and attractive environment where they can feed and set up home, raise their young and generally feel welcome and at ease.

Although not all gardeners would agree, I firmly believe that birds are some of my best gardening friends and the small amount of damage they do to my garden is far outweighed by their consumption of insects and the pleasure of their company. I protect my soft fruit with a fruit cage which spares me a lot of heart-ache and denies the birds only a small proportion of the tasty things they can feed on. (Ironically, the only trouble I've had with it came in the depths of winter, when we had the heaviest snowfall for several years and the metal frame of my fruit cage buckled under the weight. My neighbour, who is both considerably taller and stronger than me, bent it back into shape again.)

Hanging sliced onions in the bushes when the fruits are nearly ripe, or covering them with old net curtaining, will also discourage birds from eating what you don't want them to have.

Birds can be encouraged into the garden by providing them with nesting sites, water, berried shrubs (with berries which they *are* allowed to eat), food in winter and perching sites away from their own predators.

Hedges will provide birds with shelter and in many cases supplies of food. But we can help provide both of these without too much trouble.

A small piece of fat suspended from a branch in fruit trees, or from a cane stuck in the ground among the roses, will attract tits in the wintertime who, while awaiting their turn on the dangling fat,

Dangling fat attracts bluetits in winter

will tuck into overwintering aphid eggs and other tasty morsels. A bird table which keeps the food dry and protects the birds who make use of it from the unwelcome attention of cats is a real boon in any garden. A barrier fitted round the supporting pole will also prevent squirrels from stealing the nuts and other goodies put out for the birds.

Bird boxes can be bought, though they're not difficult to make and, placed on trees or attached to house walls, they will provide attractive nesting sites for tits, nuthatches and robins.

If you can, and I already have, put bat boxes in the garden. Bats are protected by law, their numbers having declined throughout the country because of the widespread use of chemical pesticides in agriculture and in house lofts. My motives are partly altruistic, to provide roosting accommodation, but in return I enjoy seeing the occupants flying at dusk and guzzling insects by the score. My bats seem happy to be living in a chemical-free corner of Yorkshire and eat as many moths, craneflies and aphids as they wish.

My greatest problem, as yet unsolved, is combating the ravenous hordes of slugs that carry out a sort of guerrilla warfare at night in the garden. This, too, has moved me to verse ... some sort of therapy, perhaps.

I am a slug.
I am slimy, I'm smug
'Cos I live in a garden – ho! ho!
I eat seedlings and flowers
Through the dark evening hours

And I gobble French beans by the row.
I can breakfast on hostas
And not count the cost as
There's plants by the dozen to chew.
I might happily munch
A fresh lettuce for lunch
And for tea I'll have brassica stew.

Oh, but night-time's the best
When I join with the rest
In consuming the pick of the crop.
Then there's loving and tenderest
Fusions of gender lest
Production of baby slugs stop!

But a warning, my friends,
There are means to our ends,
There are hedgehogs and beetles and frogs,
There are thrushes and moles,
Hungry blackbirds and voles
And a pair of inquisitive dogs.

But the worst threat of all
Is a gardener – quite small –
Who invites every slug to partake
Of a tempting, black brew
She calls beer – and, if you
Fall a victim – your life is at stake.

At night from the porch
She'll emerge with a torch
And she'll carry a pail of salt water.
Her gloved hand will stop
Hover, pluck – and then plop!
She's out on her ritual slug-slaughter.

Fellow slugs – all beware –
She's organic, I fear.
My attempts to abide here must fail.
Though the food is delicious,
This woman is vicious –
It's time I was hitting the trail …

If only they all would!
I do go slug-hunting at dusk, or by torchlight, and on damp evenings I can collect as many as a hundred at a time! During the daytime, too, we find them under the plastic lining the pathways in the vegetable garden – slugs are the bane of my life!

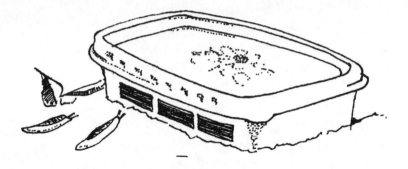

Anti-slug traps

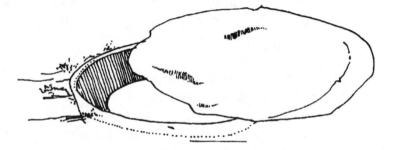

I refuse to use slug pellets but put down slug traps. My garden is dotted about with small cartons sunk into the ground, containing beer. The slugs love it and there is always a good 'catch'. Did I say 'good'? It's a revolting business and I loathe it. Unfortunately, these pests do enormous damage in my garden, so much so that I can hardly grow anything outside from seed. They demolish any new growth and it's very demoralizing, to put it mildly, to plant out new seedlings and within days find that they have vanished without trace.

Beer traps have to be emptied every few days and renewed; unless they're fitted with lids rain can dilute them to the point of being useless and, of course, it's quite an expensive business. I'm hoping to persuade my brother-in-law to make me some beer at home. It's becoming an embarrassment to buy so many cans of the cheapest beer available at the local supermarket. I fear a reputation for meanness or alcoholism, or both! I'm told that honey will work too, but the beer is so successful that I'm reluctant to switch.

I try other methods, too. I've tried placing holly leaves around plants. Slugs don't like crawling over sharp-pointed, prickly material, so in theory holly leaves should work well. In practice, however, it doesn't take long for the birds to disperse them. Lime, soot, sand, sawdust, hair clippings, horse hair, pine needles, grit – any rough material will deter slugs to some extent, but each of these needs to be renewed regularly because of dispersal by wind, rain or wildlife. Once there's a gap in your defences, the slugs will find a way through it.

Another idea for dealing with slugs is to sink plastic lawn-edging around seedlings, or any treasured plant. The soil should be level with the top of the edging on the outside of the 'trap', but trowel out a little 'moat' on the inside close to the plastic edging. Place one or two flat stones inside the fenced-off area in the hope that predator beetles will be trapped inside and will take shelter under the stones and consume any slugs they find inside their compound. The number of beetles will increase and when the seedlings are grown up a little, and are no longer as attractive to slugs, the lawn-edging can be moved elsewhere.

Aluminium sulphate can be sprinkled or made into a solution and, although not organic, it is harmless to humans, other mammals and earthworms. Its effect on slugs is to hamper their ability

to produce mucus. In desperation I have suc-
cumbed to using this, available as Fertosan Slug
Powder; all I need now is a hedgehog to enter the
lists as my champion and do battle with the foe on
my behalf. I've provided a cosy home for the winter, so I hope it will reciprocate chivalrously and
with valour. I hope it's jolly hungry too after its
hibernation, but first it will have to be imported. I
have tried to make my garden rabbit-proof and,
sadly, this means it is hedgehog-proof as well.

As you'll see from David's drawing, my hedgehog's home is really a wooden box measuring a
foot high by about 15 inches wide by a foot deep.
(The wood has to be untreated; hedgehogs won't
appreciate attempts to preserve the timber and are
very fussy about unaccustomed aromas.) To this
box is attached an entrance tunnel 4 inches high by
5 inches wide and a ventilator pipe about 15 inches
long. The sides, front and back panels can all be
nailed to the floor, but the top panel should be left
loose, so that it can be removed after the winter for
spring-cleaning (once the hedgehog has moved
out, of course).

The hedgehog box needs to be disguised under
a pile of soil or dead leaves, and a sheet of polythene placed under this covering will keep out the
worst of the winter rain, though you'll need to
make sure the ventilation pipe isn't covered by the
polythene or the camouflaged material. For the
same reason you should cover the inside end of the
pipe with wire mesh, to prevent the hedgehog's
lavish supplies of bedding material clogging it up.

There's no guarantee that a hedgehog will
accept your invitation to spend the winter in this
'des. res.', but a piece of bacon rind strategically

The hedgehog box

placed inside might entice one in. So might a supply of dry hay, which could be used for nesting.

When spring arrives, another piece of bacon rind placed in the entrance will tell you whether or not there's a hedgehog still at home. If the bacon rind remains untouched, you can safely remove the camouflage, take off the lid and clean out the box for its next resident. A herbal flea powder for dogs will sort out any of the hedgehog's own 'residents' which may have lingered behind.

A final word about hedgehogs. Those who choose not to move into your carefully prepared winter let, and others camping out at other times of the year, might settle down under a pile of garden refuse, a pile of logs or, even worse, deep in a heap destined for a bonfire. So we should always remember to check any possible hedgehog hiding-place, before disturbing it, or setting fire to it.

Another slug deterrent I have just heard of is plant pots made from newspaper. They're very satisfying, being both recycled household waste and biodegradable. You plant out seedlings in these, leaving half an inch of the pot above the soil surface. The slug finds the edge of the pot is too sharp for comfort in dry weather. Apparently the pots stay dry in wet weather too, protected by the leaves of the plant. I can't see how this could be the case with small seedlings – but I'll certainly try it.

The technique for making these newspaper pots is delightfully simple and even if they prove not to be totally successful as slug barriers, they are still useful for your seedlings in place of peat pots. All you need is a sheet of newspaper (tabloid size), a cylinder around which to roll it (something like a metal spray canister is best, or an empty sealant tube). Cut or tear a strip of paper to the height of the pot you want, plus one or two inches for the base. Roll the paper round your cylinder width-ways, leaving one or two inches overhanging at the end of the tube. Twist round this overhanging paper to make a flat base. Remove the tube and there's your pot. You don't need bottoms for them if your potting compost or leafmould is well packed at the bottom, the rest will stay in place while you plant out the pot. It couldn't be simpler!

One form of slug trap that I have successfully used is made from plastic lemonade bottles cut into sections. They make excellent mini-cloches for small plants as well as effective slug barriers.

I now have a small pool in the garden, specially created to attract frogs and toads, both blessed with hearty appetites for slugs. I already have blackbirds and thrushes – so I feel confident that this army of predators will help me reduce the slug problem to manageable proportions. After all, I am

Plastic bottle mini-cloche

providing them with a *supersafe* environment in return.

Surrounded by dry-stone walls, my garden is reasonably rabbit-proof, though I need to keep a good check for any little holes that appear from time to time and through which greedy bunnies might squeeze. They may be cute – but not in my back yard! Planting onions among the brassicas and salads (favourite rabbit food) is supposed to repel them, but rabbit-plagued friends just scoff at that notion, and say that their rabbits eat the onions too! Blood and bone meal is recommended as a deterrent and will improve your soil at the same time. I have read that the plant some of us know as 'dusty miller', and that others of us call by its hybrid name of cineraria, is said to repel rabbits.

Frogs and toads are slug predators

Cineraria 'Diamond' is both the prettiest and apparently the most effective.

My friend, Madge Hindle, is so afflicted by Rabbit 'and all Rabbit's friends and relations' that she swears they come tapping on her french windows for food, but only after they have first destroyed the garden plants. The gate and the door into my garden are, I hope, rabbit-proof, but no doubt there's a team of Yorkshire rabbits learning pole-vaulting at this very moment and sooner or later I'll be attacked, too.

Another anti-rabbit idea is to chop up an old garden hose into lengths a few feet long. These might fool the rabbits into thinking there are snakes and not fairies at the bottom of your garden – at any rate you will soon find out how cute they really are, but I am afraid that a rabbit-proof fence sunk two feet into the ground is the only sure remedy.

Pails of human urine are supposed to be an effective way of dissuading deer from coming into the garden. I wonder whether that would deter rabbits, too? There is a new product on the market, based on lion dung extract, which apparently works as a deer repellent. Fortunately, not too many of us need to worry about visitations from stags and hinds and to use it to frighten off the rabbits seems to be taking a hammer to crack a nut. Besides, I can't imagine that there are enough lions in the country to flood the market with this product – so I'll leave that one for people who really need it.

The sense of smell lies behind one of the most effective pest traps used by organic gardeners. This is the one designed to catch male codling moths. Female codling moths lay their eggs in apple and pear trees and it is these eggs that grow into the caterpillars which attack the fruit, leaving unsightly holes in it. The traps make use of an artificial pheromone, the scent that female codling moths use to attract the males. If they're hung in fruit trees towards the end of May, male moths home in on them only to become fatally adhered to a sticky board hidden inside the trap. With the males put out of commission, so to speak, significantly fewer eggs can be fertilized, and the result is fewer caterpillars to spoil the apples and pears.

Apple and pear trees can be protected from the unwanted attention of the female winter moth by means of a four-inch-wide fruit-tree grease band

Codling moth trap

placed round the trunk. The female winter moth can't fly and has to climb the trunk to her egg-laying site. The grease band catches her on her way upwards in the autumn or spring and prevents her laying the eggs that become the caterpillars which damage leaves, buds and blossom.

Other pests can be inhibited by the cunning use of barriers. I tempt providence when I say that I haven't ever suffered from the depredations wrought by the carrot fly, only, I imagine, because the organic method of control is so successful. Each year I build a barrier around the crop using a very fine mesh tied or stapled to posts. The barrier must be 24 inches to 30 inches high (the flies don't fly higher than that). In my experience the time and

Carrot fly barrier

trouble taken to construct the barrier is amply rewarded. Carrot flies are attracted to the crop by smell, which they can sense from several miles away. In fact we've now decided to build a permanent movable barrier with a side that I can let down in order to reach the crop.

Squares of carpet underlay have also proved to be a most unlikely but highly effective barrier against cabbage root fly. This lays its eggs near the stem of the plant, so that when they hatch the offspring can burrow into the ground and attack the roots. Not wishing to tempt fate, I take the precaution every year of cutting five-inch squares of carpet underlay. These are then slit from one edge to the centre, and at planting out I level off the soil and place a square around each stem. They've never failed me yet.

My broad beans have been prone to attack by blackfly and I've taken to pinching out the growing tips at the first sign of these unwelcome visitors. In fact, I usually play safe and do this before they arrive.

I don't have a greenhouse, but I've still suffered from whitefly on tomatoes and on a datura plant indoors. Bright yellow is a colour which attracts them, so a card or can could be painted bright yellow and then covered with grease to trap them once and for all.

Oak smoke does wonders in smoking salmon and the smoke from oak leaves can be of great benefit in the greenhouse. If you have problems with aphids, whitefly or ants in the greenhouse, smoke some oak leaves for about thirty minutes – not you personally, but find a suitable metal container and leave the smouldering heap to do its dirty work. The smoke will not kill soil bacteria, it isn't poisonous and it won't leave any unhealthy residue.

Alternatively *Encarsia formosa*, a minute parasitic wasp, can be ordered commercially from the HDRA and other suppliers and introduced into the greenhouse or wherever. The wasp lays its eggs inside the whitefly scale and when they hatch they eat their host – a ghoulish business, gardening!

So far I have not been troubled by ants. I find them fascinating to watch. They have a remarkably organized lifestyle, but they also have a nasty habit of cosseting aphids over winter and then carrying them back to your favourite rose trees in spring – and then, if you please, 'milking' them for their honeydew! If you are troubled by black ants, the leaves of catmint (*Nepeta*) can be strewn in their path, to deter them.

Two friends, gardening enthusiasts on the other side of the world, have problems quite different from mine. We don't have to contend with snakes and poisonous spiders as they do, but they garden virtually on a cliff-face and through scorching summer months with the odd wallaby hopping through the grapefruit trees. Peter has come up with an idea for catching fruit flies. He makes slits in the shoulder of a lidded plastic bottle through which the flies creep by the dozen to feed on a brew of water, honey and Vegemite. They are then trapped and can be subsequently removed. Vegemite is available here now, but as I'm a daily consumer of Marmite, it's in the cupboard and I'm sure it will prove to be a tasty substitute.

In the final resort there are a few pesticides and fungicides which are regarded as acceptable by organic gardening bodies, such as the HDRA. Derris and pyrethrum (usually found mixed together) are two of these. Both are extracted from plants and both kill aphids, small caterpillars and beetles on contact or if they eat them. In the case of pyrethrum, it's important to check that derris is the only substance added, if you want to use it 'organically'; other chemical additives are not acceptable in organic terms.

Derris and pyrethrum break down rapidly, so leaving no damaging residues in the soil. However, they will kill hoverflies, ladybirds, bees, frogs, toads and other 'garden helpers', so I would only use them at night to try to avoid the daytime helpers at least.

I do look on them as a last resort – I must like a challenge! It just seems a fairer treatment to encourage predators rather than going in with the big guns at the first sign of trouble.

Bacillus thuringiensis is a powdered biological control which, mixed with water, is lethal to certain

caterpillars (particularly those which affect brassicas) while leaving all other insects unharmed.

I would very much like to recommend some of
the homemade pesticides which in the past have
served organic gardeners so well, but unfortunately these have not been tested by the regulatory
authorities and so are now branded as illegal. Far
be it for me to persuade you into a life of crime, but
it seems to me to be an odd state of affairs that cigarettes, which are so injurious to health that they
carry a 'Government Health Warning', can still be
sold over the counter by the tens of thousands
daily, whereas such things as quassia, rhubarb and
nettles are condemned without trial. Of course, if
you really want to use an insecticide containing
quassia, all is not lost – you can buy it from a shop.
Bottled and sold commercially it suddenly
becomes legal again.

Here's another imponderable. Many gardeners
know that soapy water spells death and disaster to
aphids. Well, I'm afraid that now that too is illegal.
If, however, you are throwing it on the roses with
the intention of watering them – that's OK.
Apparently it's all in the mind of the waterer.
Perhaps we should issue a quick warning of '*Garde
à l'eau*' to give the greenfly time to take cover
before the deluge happens!

On the whole, organic fungicides are difficult to
find, in my experience, but good soil seems to prevent too many problems. If it is absolutely necessary it is better to use a sulphur-based fungicide
rather than any other.

As I've tried to indicate, a degree of tolerance
and a wider appreciation of natural harmony is
one of the enduring rewards of organic gardening,
even if at times of crisis and despair it may

momentarily seem like its biggest millstone. To illustrate this, perhaps a little tongue-in-cheek, I'd like to share the occasion when my garden was invaded by some totally unexpected livestock – and I use the word without inverted commas.

It was a weekend in the summer. I was giving a party for about thirty people on the Saturday. Joan, my friend from Bristol, was staying with me. With a guest who really enjoys gardening, you feel it isn't an imposition to ask for help, and together we'd made the garden look really lovely. By Thursday it looked so good that we decided we could now spend a little time indoors concentrating on the food. Our plans were going well; we were even feeling a little smug.

At six o'clock on Friday morning, my sister Veda, who'd arrived with Alastair, her husband, the night before, came into my room in what a Victorian novel might describe as a state of agitation. She'd come to tell me that I had cattle in the garden, and when I looked out five of the heifers I was used to admiring so fondly in the field next door were now repaying the courtesy on the wrong side of the wall! In the field they'd never struck me as looking particularly large; transferred to the garden they seemed like elephants.

Throwing on some old clothes and hauling Joan from her well-earned slumber I tried phoning the farmer – and got no reply. He was out milking, so there was nothing for it but to run along to the farm to fetch him, because I knew that if I tried to round up the five intruders they'd probably stampede and cause untold havoc.

They'd had a pretty good try as it was. The ground was quite damp, so their hooves had left large dents all over the grass and in the borders.

They'd managed to get everywhere and the scene of devastation was amazing to behold. One had found her way right up on to the terrace where she had succeeded in cracking one of the flagstones. If the french windows had been open I think she would probably have been into the house and upstairs for an early breakfast.

Even in the face of this scene of appalling chaos I was fascinated to see that they'd tucked into all the bushes with red leaves. A particular favourite, a cherry, had been defoliated as far as they could reach.

Manure, which I love so much, was now every-where – fresh, ripe and in none of the right places. I kept coming across deposits of it cloaking bushes.

Ernest, the farmer, was deeply apologetic. It seemed that the heifers had managed to open the field gate at the bottom of the garden by licking the wire hoop that fastened it until they'd flipped it over the stone which held it shut. He said he'd come and roll the path, which was horribly churned up, and he did so later, which was very good of him. I was hugely relieved that I'd resisted the temptation to plant a yew in the garden – deadly poisonous to cattle.

Once he'd rounded them up and returned them to the field, we had a couple of cups of good strong coffee and then set to work. Shortly afterwards drizzle set in.

On closer inspection few things in the garden had escaped unscathed. A lot were broken com-pletely. I remember quite a number of branches of low-growing *Lonicera nitida* had snapped off. We ended up just sticking them back in the soil cos-metically, knowing that they wouldn't die before

Pyramid of 'Painted Lady' runner beans showing that vegetables can look decorative.

Raised beds and fruit cage awaiting spring planting.

The vegetable end of the garden.

Pear tree weighted with small stones to control and shape its growth.

Companion planting at work – chives bordering roses.

The garden as it is today (*and opposite*), through the seasons.

The garden really comes of age – what next?

Old wheelbarrow planted entirely with spare garden seedlings.

My favourite views of the garden.

the weekend (and the party) was over. To my utter amazement they all took root!

Meanwhile, my brother-in-law hosed off all the deposits of manure. Everybody staying had a task and by mid-afternoon some semblance of order had been restored. Under the circumstances the garden was looking reasonable by the time of the party, though some of my guests may have been slightly surprised by the apparent results of my organic gardening.

That was by far the biggest disaster I've suffered to date, set against which the nibbling of the odd caterpillar pales into insignificance.

Since adversity in the garden seems to bring out the poet in me, here are a few concluding thoughts about another bane of my life when I'm gardening:

> Midges and flies,
> Midges and flies
> Crawl up my nose,
> Down my bra, in my eyes,
> They're driving me crazy,
> These flysies and midges.
> They're into my socksies
> And into my britches.
> Oh Lord! For what reason,
> In which silly season,
> Did you create midges
> And blood-sucking flies
> To creep in my niches,
> To bite at my thighs,
> Till I'm dotted with spots
> And I'm scratching my itches?
> My social life's ruined.
> I *hate* flies and midges.

7 Fruit and Vegetable Growing

'A variety of fruit and everything useful for the kitchen.'

Henry Fielding
Joseph Andrews

Like the gentleman whose garden drew those words of praise from Joseph Andrews in Fielding's novel, I am a slave to the rhythm of the seasons. The lowest ebb comes in February when my garden is at its most desolate. That's when I thank God for evergreens, and why I have a fair sprinkling of them greening up the vista, providing early nesting places for the birds and cut foliage for indoors. Some of them give flowers, too: favourites are *Viburnum bodnantense* and a much loved *Helleborus corsica*, strong, handsome and huge with masses of lime-green flowers which last for months, often from January to June.

March brings panic. Should I start sowing sweet peas early indoors? The beans? What will the weather be like? All the gardening calendars must be designed for gardens that grow south of the Wash. So I have to add three or four weeks on to the suggested dates for sowing, or potting on and planting out. I err on the safe side and plant later than advised. The soil needs to be warm and hospitable for those baby seedlings – they need cosseting.

The remainder of spring and summer is filled with hard work and excitement. Every week brings new delights as vegetables thrive. Salad comes to the table, fresh and undefiled by chemicals. The odd slug or caterpillar may have to be removed in the preparation, but their appearance is itself confirmation that the food is *safe* to eat. Who wants to eat plant material on which no other creature can live?

I now grow soft fruit in a cage. The birds used to have a bonanza in my garden, which is sometimes left undisturbed for a day or two. They'd get very angry when I came home, obviously assuming that the place was theirs. But, oh at times their songs just fill the heart with joy and I forgive them every single redcurrant and raspberry they have taken. I've reached a compromise and now I have caged fruit and they can have the bushes I've left outside the cage.

The growing season is short and so is the time I have available for harvesting. I try rather inexpertly stringing onions and garlic – I vow to master the technique for next year. I freeze the excess soft fruit, plums and pears, freeze vegetables which I can't use immediately and herbs, too.

Quite a lot of drying of herbs goes on, so late summer into autumn is still a busy time. Lots of 'muck' then gets spread and the garden is tidied for winter. Quick-burning bonfires are lit to rid the garden of debris that can't be disposed of in other ways, the ash is then added to the compost heap.

And suddenly we are into winter – and what will the robin do then, poor thing? He will still come into my garden to brighten my days. Come rain or shine I'll be finding jobs to do, and the robin will be hopping alongside, hoping I will turn up a few good grubs for him to eat.

It's wet, cold and stony. It's a slug's utopia. But it's a place where I have forged a bond with nature and where I feel honoured and privileged that nature has co-operated beyond my wildest expectations and where it bestows upon me heart's ease and tranquillity.

For the last few years I've intended to write a calendar of the jobs that need to be done in the garden each month. But that still remains no more than a good intention; my time seems to be completely filled just doing things that desperately need doing immediately. However, I have Lawrence Hills's marvellous book *Month by Month Organic Gardening*, to turn to whenever I need to check on what I should or shouldn't be doing. I also rely a great deal on two excellent books by Jim Hay, *Vegetables Naturally* and *Natural Pest and Disease Control*.

One of the most valuable ideas of organic gardening, which a rapidly growing number of gardeners have put into practice, is growing vegetables in raised beds. They're certainly extremely efficient in terms of saving space, and a lot of gardeners will appreciate the fact that once the beds are created, they are energy (human energy) saving as well.

The principal feature of raised beds is that all the work on them can be done by reaching easily from outside the bed. So there's no need to walk on them once they've been initially prepared. The follow-on from this is even more pleasing. Because there's no need to walk on the soil, it doesn't get compressed; and because it doesn't get compressed there's no need to dig it over every winter. Growing vegetables without digging becomes a

Raised bed

practical, efficient and eminently rewarding activity.

You can design raised beds to suit your own requirements. You'll need paths between the beds to give you and a wheelbarrow easy access. My raised beds are about 14 feet long by 3 feet 6 inches wide, which makes them easy enough for me to reach across. We have used old floor boards to box the beds in, but other materials can be used – be inventive and scavenge. The beds were deeply dug when they were first made and filled with good soil. Since then they've been very well fertilized and mulched, so that the soil has just got better and better from one season to the next. Crop rotation ensures that there is no build-up of soil pests and each bed can be fertilized individually for the specific needs of each crop.

Another advantage of using raised beds, which is especially appealing to anyone with a small garden, is that you can plant very much closer together than you can in conventionally cultivated vegetable gardens. So more plants are grown in less space and the plant foliage forms a canopy which helps stifle weeds and also protects the soil from heavy rain. Any weeds which do grow can be removed easily, again because the soil isn't packed down hard from being regularly walked upon.

If I have one reservation about my raised beds, it's that they can create wonderful hidey-holes for slugs. They are to be found nestling 'sluggishly' a few inches below the soil, clinging to the wooden boards. So at least we know where to look for them. But slugs do love raised beds – as much as the worms do – and dealing with them is one of my constant struggles, as the previous chapter shows.

I must allow myself a digression here to mention Esther Dean, an amazingly inventive Australian gardener I've read about. Had I known that she lived on the outskirts of Sydney, I'd have been on the telephone to her on my last holiday there to ask if I could visit her to see how she is able to garden as she does, for some of her plants grow on concrete! To be more accurate, they grow on nutritious mulches laid on concrete. Yet the results are spectacular. Whether or not all her ideas would transfer to Yorkshire, I'm not sure. But I tried her scheme of growing potatoes on hay and that was reasonably successful.

I spread the hay out as directed, added some compost, put in the potatoes and covered them with a top layer of straw. The potatoes grew quite happily in this novel bed. The crop wasn't as good as I would expect from my own raised beds, but it was a fascinating experiment and a joy to collect ready-cleaned potatoes just by lifting a chunk of straw.

I don't grow early potatoes because we don't get ours out early enough at home to make them feasible, so I just grow a main crop. I enjoy experimenting and trying different varieties, however, so I share seed potatoes with friends, who bring different seed potatoes, from their gardens. Last year I tried the variety 'pink fir apple'. They didn't produce a very big crop, but they tasted delicious and have become a regular. One thing I always do with any potatoes I grow is to put a good thick layer of chopped comfrey in the bottom of the trench. All the potatoes I've tried seem to love that, but to my cost I now realize that the comfrey must be well wilted before use – it's such a virile plant that even the leaves will form new plants if given the chance. Still, it's nice to have new comfrey plants to give to friends.

Each season my potatoes occupy a bed of their own. The brassicas go into another bed, where I grow winter cabbages, summer cabbages, red cabbage, sprouts and cauliflowers. All this in a bed 14 feet by 3 feet 6 inches means there are only a few plants of each, and inevitably I end up sticking spare ones in wherever I can find space, because I can't bear throwing anything away! Being able to plant close together helps overcome this. And with turnips, beets and carrots in particular I pull some early little ones to make room for others and they of course taste delicious. The added benefit from this is that the crops are kept going for longer, too.

I like sugar-snap peas, so they always go into my legume bed. So do mangetouts. But I don't grow many peas as such because I prefer the varieties that let you eat the whole pod. I love broad beans and grow quite a lot, so that I can freeze them. Runner beans and dwarf French beans are 'regulars' as well, and there are many unusual varieties to be found giving different coloured flowers and pods, always good to have a change.

But of all the legumes I plant, I think the sugar snaps are my favourites. They're lovely to eat very lightly cooked, or raw in salads, or even when working around the garden.

In my root garden I grow beetroot and parsnips; any space available is filled with herbs or quick-growing salads. The carrots have a little bed all of their own with the trap surrounding it to keep out the dreaded carrot fly.

The onions grow in a bed of their own, too. Red and white onions grow there together with shallots, spring onions and my beloved garlic. Though I mustn't give the impression that I stick to this rigid segregation. For example, there was a little space at the end of the onion bed this year, so in went some turnips to make use of that.

Each year I tend to put in a few catch crops of salad stuff. I always like to have a bed of misticanza, a mix of Italian salad greens which you can 'cut and come again' to provide a wonderful range of salad crops. You only need the tiniest bit of space to do this, and there will always be a little bit of salad to go with a meal for two.

There's a globe artichoke plant growing on its own, for its appearance as much as for the artichokes; it's such a handsome plant, and I grow Jerusalem artichokes close by in a permanent position.

The crops in the four principal raised beds should be rotated from one bed to another each year. I don't grow all the vegetables listed in the following table, so cheat a little here and there. Crop rotation like this is one of the gardener's, particularly the organic gardener's, principal methods of retaining soil fertility and preventing disease.

1	2	3	4
POTATOES	LEGUMES	BRASSICAS	ROOTS
Potatoes	Peas	Broccoli	Beetroot
Tomatoes	Beans	Cauliflower	Parsnips
Sweet corn	Onions	Brussels sprouts	Carrots
Marrows	Garlic	Turnip	Salsify
	Celery	Kale	
	Lettuce	Kohl rabi	
		Swede	
		Radish	

If you grow the same crops in the same ground year after year, you're likely to be depleting the soil of some nutrients, because each group of crops draws certain minerals from it. Moving them each year reduces this mineral loss.

Similarly, many soil-borne diseases that affect particular groups of plants have less chance of becoming seriously established if the plants they attack are only present for one season in four.

On the plus side, certain plants will benefit other plants, as I've already indicated. Nitrogen-fixing legumes are a good example, replenishing nitrogen in the soil for the benefit of the ones that follow – but only, of course, if the roots are left in the ground.

Given the delicious humus that I've created for the vegetables, I'm amazed that some of my fruit trees flourish in much harsher conditions. There are two pear trees, flanking the door on to the terrace, which have their roots in little more than rubble. We did our best for them, digging out a reasonable hole and filling this with soil and compost, but life can't be easy for them. I do feed them well with seaweed meal and compost or manure, and it must be due to this that both survive and bear fruit.

I have tried and failed to be very successful with apples – I now understand why. Gardening as I do at 600ft, apples don't flourish well.

A tip for fruit trees that I've found very successful is one I came across in a commercial orchard I visited a couple of autumns ago. There they'd picked goodness knows how many tons of apples without needing a ladder to reach *any* of them. This had been made possible by small lead weights attached to the branches which persuaded them to weep. I've tried the same thing on a pear tree, using, instead of lead weights, stones hung on strings (stones being my most readily available material) and they make fruit picking much easier than it might otherwise have been now the tree has become established.

Among the soft fruits I grow summer and autumn raspberries and bilberries. I love strawberries. So, alas, do the slugs and the damage they do has been so heart-breaking that I'm coming round to the idea that I'd really be better off sticking to soft fruits that they're less likely to damage. A visit to the Floriade in Holland has given me hope, however. There they were growing in somewhat elevated conditions and it might be possible to erect a metal stand with something which looks like wide guttering (spiked with a few holes for drainage) stretched between two inverted V-shaped supports about four feet high. On this would be set a growbag in which I am sure strawberries would grow very happily out of reach of even the most adventurous slugs. One could

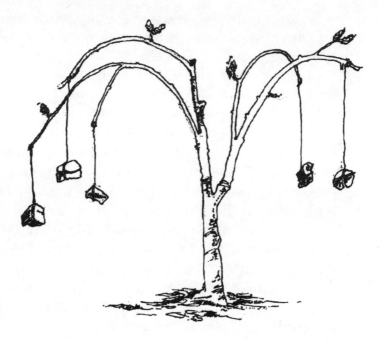

Stone weights encourage fruit trees to weep

always grease the metal legs, too, and watch and gloat! Think of the space saved – lots of room left for under-planting. Blackcurrants, whitecurrants and redcurrants suffer far less from the attentions of slugs. So maybe I will concentrate on them if the high-rise strawberries don't work.

Another idea is growing standard gooseberries. I saw these in Rosemary Verey's garden in Gloucestershire. Besides looking very elegant, the gooseberries are much easier to pick like this and you can grow other things in the ground around them. That's another good use of a small space.

Most of my fruit is either eaten fresh or frozen for use in pies or puddings. I freeze a lot of my vegetables, too. And it's always a joy to be able to share home-grown fruit and vegetables with friends and neighbours when you've got more than you can cope with yourself.

If, like me, you enjoy cooking then the sense of growing and eating the produce of your garden and labours is complete. That's why I've included a selection of my favourite recipes, to show the sort of things I enjoy preparing fresh from the garden (even if some of them come via the deep freeze).

But first a quick word about flowers in the house.

Some gardeners are very proprietorial about their flowers, and rifts are caused in otherwise harmonious relationships by one partner sneaking out at dawn and snipping roses for the table decoration that evening. These are then hidden in a cool, dark place until the dinner guests have arrived and it's too late for the gardener of the house to start a blazing row at the sight of cherished blooms gracing the dining-table. The blooms enhance the evening, praise is equally divided between cook and gardener and anger is appeased – until the next cull.

I love to have flowers from the garden and manage the year through to have some contribution from the outdoors cheering even the gloomiest of days. My sister, Veda, is creative in so many ways, one of which I'll share with you – a moss garden, which gives some purpose to the constant moss raking that takes place in my garden.

Take a dish – tureen, pie dish, even a deep saucer – in any event some container at least two inches deep, preferably three or four. Put a layer of gravel or pebbles at the bottom, then a layer of compost and finally a layer of moss. The filling should be slightly raised in the centre. Dampen the whole thing thoroughly and now make your moss garden. Flowers, snippets of shrubs, berried stems, all go into the moss and compost to make a beautiful and very long-lasting arrangement. Replace the bits that die off and keep the 'garden' going for months.

You will find sometimes that there are roots attached to the evergreen material when you pull it apart – so do it very carefully and you will have new plants to put in your garden, or give away to friends.

Now for a few ideas for the kitchen …

Veda's Scottish Supper Dish

Ingredients
8oz onions, chopped
8oz tomatoes, chopped
8oz mushrooms, chopped
8oz bacon, chopped
1oz cornflour
6oz grated cheese
2 teaspoons mixed dried herbs
1 pint milk

Method
Sauté the onions and tomatoes together. Sauté the mushrooms and bacon separately. Put them all together in an ovenproof dish with the herbs, and cover with a thick cheese sauce made by heating milk to boiling and pouring on to the cornflour which has been mixed with a little milk taken from the pint. Return this to the pan and heat it back to a simmer. Stir constantly, simmering for 3–4 minutes with cheese added.

Pour over the vegetables and bacon in the dish. Sprinkle extra cheese on top. Then cook in a moderate oven for 30–40 minutes.

This dish freezes well.

Hot Coleslaw

Ingredients
2 carrots (coarsely grated)
1 large cabbage (red or white, shredded finely)
1 onion (finely chopped)
1 small green pepper (finely chopped)

Dressing
1 cup of oil
1/2 cup sugar
1 heaped teaspoon celery seeds
1 teaspoon mustard (ready made)
1/2 cup of cider vinegar

Method
Put all the dressing ingredients in a saucepan and bring slowly to the boil. Pour the lot immediately over the mixed salad vegetables. Chill for 24 hours to marinate, turning from time to time. Drain and serve.

This salad will keep well for several days in the fridge and will even freeze.

Celery and Fennel Salad with Gorgonzola Dressing

Ingredients
1 fennel bulb (trimmed and sliced thinly)
2 sticks celery, chopped finely

4–6 button mushrooms, sliced
6 radishes, sliced
2 tablespoons each of chopped spring onion,
parsley and chives
Lettuce
Combine the ingredients.

Dressing
1 teaspoon fresh lemon juice
2 tablespoons olive oil
1/2 teaspoon French mustard
Salt and pepper
3oz Gorgonzola cheese

Method
Make a dressing from all the ingredients, except
the cheese. When the dressing is ready, add and
stir the cheese, breaking it up with a fork. Put
the salad ingredients on lettuce leaves in a salad
bowl, pour over the dressing and serve.

Carrot and Orange Salad Ring

Ingredients
1 packed unsweetened jelly (orange or lemon)
2 tablespoons white wine vinegar
1lb carrots (grated or very finely chopped)
Coriander, fresh (optional)
Juice and finely grated peel of orange (or
lemon)

Method
Make the jelly as instructed on the packet, but
using 3/4 pint of water, or water and white wine.
When cool, add vinegar, add grated carrot and

chopped coriander, lemon (or orange juice) and grated rind, stir well and leave to set in the fridge.

Beetroot and Apple Jelly Ring

Ingredients
1 packet raspberry jelly (or redcurrant)
$1/2$ pint boiling water
$1/4$ pint vinegar
2 tablespoons lemon juice
2oz shredded walnuts
1lb cooked, diced beetroot
2 eating apples, peeled, cored and finely sliced
Watercress garnish

Method
Dissolve the jelly in hot water. Cool and mix in the vinegar and lemon juice. Place the walnuts in the base of a 2-pint ring mould. Add beetroot and apple in layers. Pour on liquid jelly. Leave in a cold place to set. Unmould and garnish with watercress.

Fresh Green Sauce for Fish

Ingredients
A handful of parsley (washed and dried in a tea towel)
A handful of sorrel (washed and dried in a tea towel)
Salt and pepper to taste
250g (8oz) plain yoghurt or fromage frais

Method
Whizz together in the blender – serve cold. This

would be sufficient for 2 people – increase quantities according to need. This is particularly good with salmon – the colours look superb together. It tastes very fresh and is blissfully quick to prepare.

Garlic Olives

Ingredients
Black olives
Garlic
Olive oil

Method
Slice the peeled garlic cloves finely and pack these, along with the olives, into a screw-top jar. Cover with olive oil. Leave to marinate for a few days. Drain before serving, but save the oil to use in salad dressings.
I first had these in Spain and copied the idea when I came home. The garlic olives will keep indefinitely, if always covered with oil.

Raspberry Vinegar

Ingredients
$1/2$ lb of raspberries
1 pint white wine vinegar
8oz sugar

Method
Pour the vinegar over the raspberries and leave in a cool place for 4–5 days. Add sugar, bring to the boil in a saucepan. Simmer for 15 minutes. Cool, sieve and bottle. It's a delicious vinegar to use in salad dressings.

Herb vinegars

To make herb vinegars, use white wine or apple cider vinegar, warmed slightly and poured on lightly bruised herbs. Leave this mixture in a glass jar on a window sill in the sun and give it a shake every day. After about 2 weeks, strain it and try it for taste. If you prefer a stronger tasting vinegar, repeat the process. When you are happy with the result, strain again, add fresh herbs and use.

Garlic, rosemary, fennel, tarragon, thyme, lovage – almost any herb can be used to produce a pleasing herb vinegar.

Herbal oils

Herbal oils are even easier to make than herb vinegars.

Pour light-flavoured oils on to freshly gathered herbs in a clean glass jar. Put this on a sunny window sill for 2 weeks, covered. Stir each day. Two weeks later, strain and check for taste. Repeat the process if a stronger flavour is needed. Add fresh herbs and use.

These make good personal gifts for friends, made special by the fact that you can add the comfortingly safe words 'organically grown herbs' on your labels.

Danish Peasant Girl with Veil (Apple Dessert)

Ingredients
$1^1/2$lb cooking apples
4oz brown sugar
3oz butter

4oz fine brown breadcrumbs
$1/2$ pint thick cream or fromage frais, or
yoghurt
1oz plain chocolate

Method
Peel, core and chop the apples. Cook them
gently in a little water, with sugar to taste, until
they are soft. Purée. Melt the butter in a large
frying-pan, pour in the breadcrumbs mixed
with 3oz of sugar and stir *constantly* over a low
heat until mid-brown – they soon burn, so keep
the breadcrumb mixture moving.

Turn out on to a plate to form a ring and
allow it to cool. Spread the apple mixture in the
centre, cover with whipped cream and add
grated chocolate on top.

Parsnip Cake

Ingredients
12oz plain wholemeal flour (or a mixture of
wholemeal and white)
1 teaspoon baking powder
1 teaspoon bicarbonate of soda
1 teaspoon ground cinnamon
$1/2$ teaspon ground ginger
$1/2$ teaspoon salt
6oz sugar

tablespoons oil (a light unflavoured oil is best)
2 eggs
6oz shredded parsnip
3oz apple sauce
1 teaspoon vanilla essence
6oz chopped walnuts and hazelnuts, mixed

Method

Sift the flour with the raising agents, spices and salt into a large mixing bowl, then stir in the sugar. Make a well in the centre of these dry ingredients and add the oil, eggs, parsnip, apple sauce and vanilla essence. Beat the mixture well for 2 or 3 minutes, then stir in the nuts.

Grease a 9-inch square shallow cake tin and bake for 35–45 minutes at 180°C, 350°F or gas Mark 4. Test, and if the cake springs back when gently pressed with the finger it is cooked. Leave a few minutes then turn out on to a cake rack to cool before covering it with cream cheese icing.

Cream Cheese Icing

Ingredients
8oz cream cheese (use low fat cream cheese)
4oz butter
3 tablespoons icing sugar (sifted)
4 tablespoons sour cream
$1/2$ teaspoon vanilla essence

Method
Beat cheese and butter together. When smooth add icing sugar gradually, beat for a minute or two, add sour cream and vanilla essence. Combine and spread on the cake.

Crystallized Angelica

Ingredients
$1/2$ lb angelica stalks
8oz sugar

Method
Wash angelica stalks – cut into 3-inch lengths.
Boil in water until tender. Drain, remove any
tough outer skin. Cover with the sugar and
leave covered for 2 days.

Return to the pan with $1/2$ pint of water.
Bring to the boil, stirring constantly. Simmer
gently until the syrup has been absorbed, by
which time the angelica stalks should have a
clear appearance. Drain and cool.

Spread on a cake rack and sprinkle more
sugar over them to coat. Leave out until
completely dry, then store in airtight containers.

Blackcurrant Jam

Ingredients
6lb sugar
2 pints water
4lb blackcurrants (weighed after topping and
tailing)

Method
Boil the sugar in the water until it throws up
large bubbles and is clear. Then add the
currants. Boil for 20 minutes or until the setting
stage is reached. Remove the scum and pour
into warmed jars when a little cooled. Seal as
usual.

Pickled Nasturtium Seeds

Ingredients
Green nasturtium seed pods
Brine to cover (4oz salt to each pint of water)

Onion, finely chopped
French tarragon, chopped
$^1/_2$ pint white wine vinegar
1 blade of mace or $^1/_2$ teaspoon of powdered
mace
1 teaspoon salt
12 peppercorns
A pinch of nutmeg
A pinch of paprika

Method
Soak the nasturtium seed pods for two days in
brine, then drain, dry and layer in a clean jar
with finely chopped onion and French tarragon.
Boil together the white wine vinegar with the
seasonings.

Cool, strain and fill the jar with this liquid,
Cover, refrigerate and use after one week.
Adjust the quantity of pickling vinegar
according to the amount of available seeds.

These can be used like capers or as a
piquant addition to salads; once the jar is
opened, the contents should be used up quickly.

Autumn Chutney

Ingredients
1lb stoned plums
1lb apples (peeled and cored)
1lb tomatoes
1lb onions
1lb sultanas
1 pint vinegar
1 clove garlic (peeled and chopped)
$^1/_2$ teaspoon each: mace and mixed spice

1oz ground ginger
1lb Demerara sugar

Method
Coarsely chop the fruit and vegetables. Put them in a large pan with all the other ingredients (except the sugar). Simmer until they are tender, then add the sugar, stirring until it is dissolved. Cook until the mixture is thick. Allow it to cool and pour it into warm jars. Seal as usual.

Elderflower and Elderberry Wine

Aromatic and delicious, these are good for colds and coughs. They are my two favourite home-made wines.

Elderflower wine is light and rich with a strong flavour of muscatel. The wine of the berry is dark red and can taste very 'porty' if well made. It is also helpful in the treatment of colds, sore throats, constipation and rheumatism (in case you are looking for a medicinal excuse to pour yourself a glass of this nectar).

Elderflower Wine

Ingredients
1 pint elderflowers
3lb sugar
1 gallon water
$1/2$–1oz yeast (fresh or dried)
Citrus juice (lemon, orange or grapefruit) – optional

Method

Wash the elderflowers and remove them from the stalks. This is a picky business; try forking them off.

Simmer the florets in water for 10 minutes. Cool slightly and add the sugar. Stir well until the sugar is dissolved. When this reaches blood heat add the yeast. Cover with a couple of layers of muslin, tied tightly down to keep vinegar fly at bay. I use a sterilized plastic container for this part of the process and place it in a warm spot for 5–10 days while fermentation takes place, stirring it well with a wooden spoon twice daily.

When fermentation has subsided, strain the liquid through a jelly bag or muslin into a gallon jar, fit a fermentation lock and keep it in a warm place. Check it from time to time and rack it once a month.

For this you'll need another sterilized gallon jar on a lower level than the full one. You'll also need a length of plastic tubing about three feet long. Place one end in a full jar and suck up a little of the wine into the tube. Press the tube tightly and put the outer end into the lower container. The wine flows into this jar, and with care the sediment can be left behind in the top jar. Again fit a fermentation lock and return to the same warm place. When the fermentation has ceased altogether, the wine is ready for bottling.

Campden tablets should be used to sterilize every bit of equipment each time it is used. If all has gone well, the wine should be clear and can now be bottled, corked and labelled, and kept in a cool place.

Elderberry Wine

Ingredients
3lb fresh elderberries
3lb sugar
1 gallon water
$^1/_2$–1oz yeast (fresh or dried)

I make elderberry wine following the method I've
described for making elderflower wine.
Try them both, they're delicious.

Balm Melissa (Lemon Balm) Wine

Ingredients
4oz lemon balm leaves
3lb sugar
1 gallon water
$^1/_2$–1oz yeast (fresh or dried)

Method
This is a tonic helpful for headaches, nervous
tension and sleeplessness. It can be made in the
same way as elderflower and elderberry wine
but, if you don't want to go into the wine
business, use the lemon balm leaves to make a
soothing hot drink by pouring boiling water
over a few leaves in a teapot and leaving for
four or five minutes before drinking with added
honey, or leave until it's cold. If you then put it
in the fridge, add ice and a sprig of mint, you
have a refreshing summer drink – add some gin
too if you feel the need of a little extra
stimulation.

8 Companion Planting

'Adversity makes strange bedfellows.'
English proverb

Although I like to see the vegetable garden looking well-organized, I am attracted to the idea of mixed planting – growing vegetables and salads among the flowers and shrubs. I can see that there is an advantage in doing this. In a bed devoted to only one type of plant, should a pest attack the infestation will spread easily, as will a fungal disease. But if the food plants are interspersed with a variety of other plants, there will be less likelihood of mass infestation.

But there must be problems in this method, I think. I'm sure I would lose sight of the vegetables in the shade of the delphiniums and lupins! Also the plants would almost certainly have different nutritional needs. No, I think I will stay happily with my raised beds, thank you.

In my opinion there is, though, a lot of good sense and practical advantage to be gained in companion planting. There are many plants that can enhance the health and growth of their neighbours. Some can repel insects by their odour and others are devious underground killers dealing death and destruction, quite selectively, by their root secretions. Never let us underestimate the power of plant life! Nor do I underestimate the knowledge and experience of Alan Gear, the Chief Executive of the HDRA, and I know that he doesn't agree with me about companion planting. So maybe it's a woman's instinct which leads me to believe it's possible. Anyway, I will pass on some of the information I have gleaned and you may like to put it to the test.

There are some excellent books to be found on this absorbing subject (I've mentioned some under Further Reading on page 205), and to whet your appetite I will mention a few of the extraordinary, sophisticated things that plants are said to achieve.

There are nitrogen-fixing plants like clover and legumes, which can change atmospheric nitrogen into compounds and proteins, the form in which nitrogen can be used by other plants as well as themselves.

Borage will not only give us beautiful blue flowers and cucumber-flavoured leaves for salads and drinks, but makes an extra contribution to the soil by providing calcium and potassium. Buckwheat also provides calcium and is good for overwintering and digging in as a green manure – the ideal way to use garden space in the winter and benefit the following year's crops at the same time.

However, we have all at some time lived with, worked with, or been close to people with whom we have had an uneasy relationship and when that condition endures, the ability of both parties to live and function normally is steadily impaired.

Why do we imagine that plants are different? Because we are human beings and therefore more complex?

Not at all! We are of the same source. By becoming gardeners we are choosing to do some of nature's work for her. We try to grow plants in our garden which would never thrive together in a natural environment. We provide the right soil, location and food – but do we ever think about their social lives? I'm not suggesting that as darkness falls there are great shenanigans in the vegetable plot, or family rows in the rockery, but definitely some plants live together more happily than others. This is something I have felt instinctively, but now I know *why*.

Plants and animals are active living protoplasm, between 95 and 98 per cent of which is oxygen, carbon, hydrogen and nitrogen. In green plants there are also small quantities of sulphur, zinc, manganese, phosphorus, boron, iron, calcium, chlorine, magnesium, molybdenum and copper, all of which perform very important functions. Some plants, having extracted from the soil the elements necessary to their health and growth, then excrete certain substances from their roots, which from analysis have proved to be antibiotic and fungicidal.

Now, your humble foxglove is not providing this protein for its neighbours, it's looking after its own interests, but in so doing it's having beneficial effects on the surrounding vegetation. The healthier your plants, the more secretions from their roots, which makes another compelling argument for getting the soil into good condition and for pursuing a policy of mixed planting. Just reaching for a bottle of chemicals can never be as safe and as effective as nature's selective, gentle and highly developed wisdom.

❁ GOOD COMPANIONS

❁ *Alliums – Onion family and ornamental alliums*

Plant near roses to protect them from aphids. The one haven in my garden which I can guarantee will be slug-free is the onion bed. So this year I am planting ornamental alliums in every available space – and *hoping*!

Garlic, wonderful garlic, will discourage mice, too. So plant it among lilies and other bulbs to discourage these hungry creatures.

❁ *Basil*

Basil is a good friend to the tomato, in the garden as well as the kitchen. The flavours are truly complementary, one to the other, but if planted together the basil helps the tomato to resist insects and disease and improves its health and flavour. It is a good companion to asparagus, too.

❁ *Beans*

Plant summer savory among the beans. Some years ago I threw some marigold seeds down in a spot which I thought needed brightening up. I have long since changed my scheme for that bit of garden, but each year twenty or thirty self-seeded marigolds (very ordinary pot marigolds) pop up in the same plot. I haven't the heart to throw them out, so I transplanted them to the bean and pea raised bed and there they look very attractive, though, as I've said elsewhere, I think a better companion for the legumes is the marigold (*Tagetes*).

Nasturtium, spearmint or southernwood planted among broad beans is said to deter black-fly, but pinching out the tips seems a more certain measure to take.

❁ *Birch (Betula)*

This tree is a good companion for compost heaps because it excretes root substances which help fermentation. Keep a distance of at least six feet between the two.

❁ *Cabbages, cauliflowers and other brassicas*

Hyssop, wormwood, southernwood and thyme help to repel cabbage-white butterfly. Planting sage, rosemary, mint or celery nearby will be beneficial to the brassica family. However, do not plant with strawberries, tomatoes and runner beans.

❁ *Carrots*

Carrots love growing with tomatoes, rosemary, sage, onions and leeks. They'd be good in a casserole together, too. Don't grow them with dill, though.

❁ *Celery*

Celery loves to grow with leeks, cauliflowers, cabbage and tomatoes – another tasty casserole.

❁ *Chives*

Chives can be grown close to gooseberries and cucumbers to discourage powdery mildew, or near apple trees for apple scab.

❂   *Coreopsis (Calliopsis)*

This is useful in the garden as an insect repellent. Grow it near your favourite plants, the ones that are usually the favourites of the pests, too.

❂   *Corn (Sweet corn)*

Sweet corn lives happily with peas, beans and potatoes and gives welcome shade to members of the cucumber family.

❂   *Cucumbers*

Cucumbers like peas, radishes and sunflowers, but they must not be planted close to potatoes or aromatic herbs.

❂   *Dill*

Grow this close to cabbage but not near carrots.

❂   *Elderberry*

This is a good tree to have near the compost heap; and think of the delicious wine and cordial you can make from its fruit and flowers. If you are musical, you can even make a pipe from its hollow stems, too.

❂   *Fennel*

So beautiful, so useful as a flavouring or garnish, and as a tea with mint very soothing in digestive disorders, fennel is *not* popular with its fellows. So, plant it at a good distance from the vegetable garden. It's certainly pretty enough to go in any herbaceous border or in a large pot on the terrace.

● *Fern (bracken)*

Apart from its protective use over the delicate crowns of plants in the winter, saving them from the ravages of frost, fern leaves have a high percentage of potassium – excellent for the compost heap. The dried leaves can be powdered and are effective against 'damping-off' (just sprinkle over the potting compost), or the spent leaves can be used as a mulch. I am going to try them on my strawberry bed this year, instead of straw.

Beech trees and ferns inhibit one another's growth, but fern compost is useful in the germination of tree seedlings.

● *Feverfew* (Chrysanthemum parthenium)

My sister's migraine attacks have been subdued since she has been taking feverfew tablets and I think many sufferers grow this herb in their gardens and make a beneficial tea from its dried flowers. It is also considered to be an insect repellent and is a charming plant to have in the garden.

● *Foxglove*

The drug made from this plant is powerful and should only ever be used by professional practitioners. But a solution from foxgloves or a couple of the flowers put in a vase of other blooms will keep them fresh.

It is also helpful to the plants which grow nearby in its garden position. I have in the past, in my ignorance, thrown out these beautiful and protective plants, which seed themselves so readily – but never again. In fact I am now planting seeds of multicoloured foxgloves. They are quite exotic once one takes the trouble to look at them really carefully, and as part of a mixed planting their tall spires add grace and dignity to the scene.

❀   *Fruit trees*

Grow nasturtiums, alliums, southernwood or stinging nettles nearby. A ring of chives or garlic planted around the tree base is a good idea and helps to prevent boring insects – I know there's a joke there somewhere, but I must get on …

❀   *Garlic*

Garlic seems to me to be associated with summer holidays in Italy, so it surprises me when I harvest my crop of home-grown garlic which lasts me through the year until the next crop is ready.

I still have to master the clever way onions and garlic are plaited into strings, but I get immense pleasure every year from growing this health-giving vegetable – or do we call it a herb?

My bulbs were originally bought from the HDRA and now I replant cloves from stock each autumn, although invariably a dozen extra plants will sprout here and there, where an odd bulb has escaped being garnered in the previous year.

As well as being indispensable in the kitchen, garlic used to be made into and used as an excellent

anti-aphid spray. Roses and tomatoes love it growing nearby, but peas and beans, which should
know better, don't.

Medicinally, garlic is a prince among herbs, being
antiseptic and antibiotic, and a preserver of life, with
many centenarians attributing their longevity and
vitality to the daily munching of garlic. This doesn't
need to be considered anti-social either. Chewing
parsley or a coffee bean is reputed to dispel the
odour of garlic-scented breath, but if we all ate it
every day, there'd be no problem anyway.

The flavour of garlic grown organically is much
more intense. Its health-giving properties are more
effective, too, because of a chain reaction of enzyme
activity in the bulb which is dependent on assimil-
able sulphur produced in the soil by micro-organisms, most importantly tiny fungi which can only be
present in humus-rich soils. If you grow your food
relying on chemicals, I'm afraid you are losing out.

● *Horsetail* (Equisetum arvense)

This is a plant that intrigues me. I don't have it in my
garden, but I have 'marked' two or three sites where
it grows, because horsetail is marvellous at
combating various types of fungus. I believe it can
become a menace if allowed to proliferate, so I feel
rather smug that I know where I can lay hands on a
good supply, without being plagued by a take-over.

Horsetail is in fact one of the oldest plants
known to man and on that point alone it deserves
our respect. It is also a healing herb and before it
became illegal to engage in a spot of garden 'do-it-
yourself' made a most effective spray against powdery mildew. This ancient plant is also a handy
herb to have on a picnic. It has a high level of silica,

which is very useful in the scouring of pots and pans, so a word of advice – always pitch camp near a patch of horsetail!

❁ *Ingenuity*

Companion planting is largely a question of using one's ingenuity. Nudging nature a little this way and that, is part of an organic gardener's armoury and employing plants to do our dirty work for us presents no qualms.

Many strongly scented herbs will act as repellents. Rue, sage, thyme, eucalyptus, scented geraniums, pyrethrum, lavender, tansy and elder act as a defence – plant them freely among flowers and vegetables.

❁ *Leeks*

Leeks enjoy being planted with onions, or celery and carrots.

❁ *Lettuce*

Lettuce is happy growing with onions, carrots, cucumbers, radishes and strawberries. It sounds like a good salad to me.

❁ *Lovage*

Lovage is a most handsome, succulent plant. I have to state that the colossus which grows in my garden is about eight feet in height. I love its dark, bronze-green young foliage and the scent of celery as I jungle trek my way past it to the shed.

I use lovage in soups and casseroles, either the

leaves or the seeds, and out of the kindness of its heart it improves the health and efficacy of other plants growing nearby. What a winner!

● *Marigold*

Here's a hard worker in the garden. Not content with providing golden-orange flowers, the roots of the *Tagetes* marigold excrete substances which if planted in succession, and through several seasons (and this is something which I am at this moment putting to the test), are reputed to deter ground elder, bindweed and ground ivy.

The pot marigold (calendula) is the one used in cooking. Its petals can be scattered on salad, used to flavour soups, or added to a cake mixture.

● *Marjoram*

This is another herb which improves the health and flavour of plants growing nearby.

● *Mint*

Mint is very aromatic and so is useful as an insect repellent. It will also repel rats and mice and indoors it can be useful as a moth deterrent. It is good to plant near tomatoes and cabbage.

● *Nasturtiums*

These deserve a medal. The leaves and flowers look and taste delicious in salads. The seeds can be used as capers. They are beneficial grown near potatoes, radishes, cabbages, cucumbers, broccoli and apple trees. Even in a greenhouse a plant or two will help to repel white fly invasion. The vibrant flowers will tumble from your hanging baskets, climb your conifer or scramble along as ground cover – surely no single plant can do more!

❁ *Nettles*

Find a spot to have a patch of nettles and you will have butterflies too; the peacock and the small tortoiseshell know a good thing when they see it and choose this as the only food for their caterpillars. Put nettles (before they've flowered or seeded) on to the compost heap and you will help fermentation. Nettles are one of the plant world's great vital forces; look around where you see them growing naturally and you will notice how luxuriant is the surrounding vegetation, how free from disease and pest destruction.

Nettles in the bath, or at least an infusion of nettles added to the bath, alleviate aching limbs. Use nettles as a hair rinse or tonic, or nettles as a liquid fertilizer.

Nettles should be awarded the highest honours in the land (as I hope I have already convinced you, having dealt with them in greater detail earlier on) but they're despised by most people as a nasty, vicious, weedy thing that must be uprooted and eliminated. You and I know better – long live the nettle.

❁ *Onions*

Cabbage, tomatoes, lettuce, beets, strawberries, parsnips and carrots all live happily with onions and any member of the family *Allium*, which includes garlic.

❁ *Parsley*

Parsley is another protector and plant improver. Tomatoes, carrots, asparagus and roses will suffer fewer attacks from pests if you plant parsley near to them. And what a useful herb it is in the kitchen, so health-giving, too.

❁ *Peas*

You can plant peas in the vicinity of almost all vegetables other than members of the onion family, or gladioli. At the end of their life they will be an invaluable addition to the compost heap.

❁ *Pine*

Pine needles make a good mulch for acid-loving plants and strawberries relish a *feed* of pine needles. I would imagine the slugs aren't too keen to crawl about on them, so maybe their benefit in the strawberry bed could be twofold.

❁ *Poppy*

Poppies are heavy feeders but they can be used almost anywhere as companion plants to crowd out less attractive weeds. They are certainly an attractive alternative sometimes.

❁ *Potatoes*

Potatoes make good neighbours for corn, aubergine and cabbage. Horseradish is beneficial to the potato – but have a care, it can take over the whole plot!

Not such good friends of the potato are

tomatoes, cucumbers, raspberries and sunflowers. But a very neat two-way benefit is in operation if you plant beans with potatoes. They each protect the other from pests.

❀ *Pyrethrum*

Please find a place in your garden for these beautiful flowers. The powder is used as an insecticide and the fresh flowers will keep baddies at bay and protect surrounding plants to some extent.

❀ *Radish*

Radishes are good companions for members of the cucumber family, beans, lettuce, spinach, carrots and parsnips, but not for brussels sprouts, cabbage and cauliflowers.

❀ *Rose*

Once more our allies the onions, and all members of their family, will help to protect roses against attacks of aphids, blackspot and mildew. At one time I grew several roses together in a small oval bed on the terrace and surrounded them with chives. It looked very pretty and in fact the roses did not suffer from disease and aphids as much as others in a different part of the garden.

Parsley is another effective protector – but I still think the Limnanthes (poached egg plants) are the best of all. Soon after the buzzing of the hoverfly above their sunny, open-faced flowers, I know that the end of the aphids is in sight. The offspring of these harmless-to-humans wasp-like creatures will have a good start in life feeding on the destructive aphids.

Another herb which can be planted close to roses is rue – the grey-blue delicately fine foliage is most attractive as a border plant.

❂ *Rue*

Shakespeare mentions so many herbs in his sonnets and plays, it would be interesting to collect them all into a garden. I have never been as ambitious as that, but having played Ophelia many years ago I try to keep the herbs she mentions in my garden. Among those is rue, and once I had grown a plant of rue I have never been without it. Rue has such a singular colour, form and scent. The flowers are fairly insignificant but of an acid, yellow hue and I find it a splendid foil, especially for white flowers in indoor arrangements. Insects find the scent repellent, so it rarely suffers from infestation and seems to pass on this protection to its neighbours.

❂ *Sage*

The strong scented sage confuses the carrot fly and the cabbage white butterfly. So it is useful to plant alongside these two vegetables. In the herb garden, plant it near rosemary – they will be good for one another and will reward you for your thoughtfulness by becoming handsome, healthy small shrubs.

❂ *Southernwood* (Artemisia abrotanum)

Southernwood is another plant I always have and will always want in my garden. Crush the feathery foliage as you pass by and the most evocative, 'old-fashioned' scent clings to your fingers. It is one of the first plants I can remember, is useful in pot-pourri or as a moth deterrent, and guards your trees and cabbages from the worst ravages of moths and caterpillars.

❁ *Strawberries*

Strawberries grow happily with lettuce, spinach and beans.

❁ *Tansy*

This is a pungent herb that spreads itself with great generosity! Flies, ants, most flying insects, beetles and bugs are repelled by tansy and it is helpful when planted near fruit trees, soft fruits and roses. It's also another goody for the compost heap.

❁ *Tea leaves*

I know we don't grow a lot of tea in the Dales, but tea leaves have their part to play in companion planting. They're always welcome in the compost heap or dug in around acid-loving plants. And you can mix carrot and radish seeds with your spent tea leaves to prevent maggots.

❁ *Tomatoes*

Tomatoes can be planted with asparagus, basil, gooseberries, carrots, onions, parsley, chives, roses, garlic, marigolds and nasturtiums. They are not compatible with the brassicas and fennel, corn and potatoes.

Smokers, beware: you can transmit disease to your tomatoes if you handle them with smoky fingers.

● *Turnips*

Turnips and peas are helpful to one another. Wood ash is useful sprinkled around the plants to control scab.

● *Valerian*

Valerian grows abundantly in my garden. I keep trying to persuade it to grow in crevices in the dry-stone walls – so far without success. But as it has the ability to enhance the growth and performance of its close companions, because it stimulates phosphorus activity, perhaps it is more useful left where it is.

● *Wallflowers*

Plant these under apple trees for better yields.

● *Wormwood* (Artemisia absinthium)

The greatest assistance that wormwood can give to other plants seems to be repelling various insects: moths, fleas, flea-beetles and cabbage white butterflies. It also holds back the development of several herbs, including sage, fennel and coriander.

I think I would find another of its uses somewhat discouraging, too. It is an ingredient in the making of absinthe, the liqueur which, it is reputed, damages the brain. If you really want it in your garden (and in my first herb garden I had a

wormwood plant) plant it somewhere Garbo-like –
alone.

❁   *Yarrow*

Fortunately yarrow grows easily, almost
everywhere. It is an essential plant in a mixed lawn
where its pretty flowers and furry leaves, colour
and scent can be enjoyed, though its extravagant
growth can be curbed by mowing regularly.

Yarrow is a plant of immense generosity, giving
out healing root secretions which strengthen its
neighbours and enables them to be more resistant
to disease. Herbs benefit if a few plants of yarrow
are growing nearby, their scents, flavours and oils
becoming more intense. A splendid liquid fertilizer
can be produced from the plant, which contains
chlorides of potash, phosphates, copper, nitrates
and lime – it's good for your compost, too. Take a
handful of yarrow to a pint of boiling water, allow
it to cool and then strain. Dilute the yarrow fluid
with four parts of water as soon as possible after
making. This makes a marvellous foliar feed or
root fertilizer.

9 A Walk Around Ryton Gardens

'All Nature seems at work.'

Samuel Taylor Coleridge
'Work Without Hope'

I love to see other people's gardens and Joan, my gardening friend from Bristol, and I try to have a garden-visiting holiday together most years.

One of my favourites is Ryton Gardens at Ryton-on-Dunsmore, near Coventry. This is no ordinary garden. You won't see great sweeps of lawn, mature shrubberies and archways of laburnum, gazebos, ha-has or orangeries. For the main purpose here is not to be decorative or pretty-pretty. This is a garden of ideas and ideals.

The Henry Doubleday Research Association (HDRA) is a registered charity and was originally based in Essex, but since 1985 it has been here at Ryton, where it is accessible to many more people, and this move to the centre of the country has proved to be phenomenally successful.

The new location, combined with a rapidly developing interest in conservation and concern for the environment, has almost overwhelmed the dedicated workforce at Ryton Gardens. The Chief Executive and the Executive Director, Alan and Jackie Gear, are now dear and valued friends for whom I have great respect and admiration of their unceasing hard work in the promotion of organic methods of gardening.

There have been three series on Channel 4 centred on the gardens and methods of growing at Ryton. Two were called *All Muck and Magic* and the third *Loads More Muck and Magic* – you may have seen them. The titles reflect a tongue-in-cheek attitude to many people's view of organic gardening, but there is nothing fey about these people at Ryton; they are scientists involved in research into the most effective and safe methods of producing food crops and gardening naturally by following a chemical-free method. So let me take you with me to Ryton and tell you of the interesting and informative time one can spend there.

The land was originally a riding school establishment; the site is windswept and since the organization has been there, they have planted over 5,000 hedging plants to give protection to the growing area.

There is first of all a composting and fertilizing display. Always the soil comes first and here they show us various methods of making compost; commercial bins, New Zealand boxes, compost tumblers and a covered heap. There's also a worm bin for tiny gardens where beautiful worm compost can be made out of kitchen waste.

Near to this we will see leafmould being created and a display of green manure plants similar to the ones I've mentioned previously. What would an organic garden be without a comfrey bed? Well, here is comfrey growing a-plenty, being used as a mulch and as a feed for tomatoes and all the pot-grown plants.

With the current search to find a substitute for peat there's a display at Ryton of organic growing materials which can be used as substitutes. This includes coir (coconut fibre), which I have often used for seed trays and transplanting and which I have found clean to use and very effective – even if maybe it has a tendency to dry out rather quickly. The soil in the greenhouse border is planted up with fenugreek to keep it active over the winter months.

We then cross the lawn and come to a pretty impressive display of herbs. This seems to look attractive all the year round and gives a good example of planting that may depend more on its leaf shape and scent than on its flowers.

I have a soft spot always for allotments. I love passing them in the train and seeing the great variety of sheds and planting that make up the average allotment – such individuality, such character. Well, Ryton doesn't let us down. There's an allotment split into four parts to demonstrate crop rotation in practice, along with a comfrey bed, a compost bin and a leafmould container. They also demonstrate methods of pest control used by organic gardeners and although the children's play area is next door to it, I don't think there's any intentional connection!

Leave the children in the play area and walk along the shrub border. There's nothing too exotic or out-of-the-way here, just a good example of low maintenance gardening with plants giving constant interest, and you will notice a woodchip mulch among the shrubs. This achieves two objectives: it acts as a weed-suppressing mulch and improves and feeds the soil with organic matter.

Now we will reach a wildlife conservation area where there is a pond, some native woodland and a beautiful wildflower meadow. Charming, you may think, and so it is, but there's method in the organic gardener's madness. Here is the workforce of the garden. These habitats have been created to attract a great variety of predators to the garden. Predators need pests as food and pests need to be got rid of. It's all very neat and satisfactory.

There is a display of an ornamental kitchen garden with formally trained soft fruits. When folk have only a small plot and yet want to make the most of it by growing some edible produce, it's hard to know the best way to go about it – but here are ideas galore.

Next on the visit is the 'No Dig Vegetable Garden' which will have a lot of devotees. As I've said, this subscribes to the theory that a considerable amount of damage is done to the soil structure by digging, and once again there is a four-course crop rotation in use. The potatoes are planted with a bulb-planter then mulched generously with hay and lawn mowings. A friend from Bristol visibly reeled the first time he visited Ryton and saw how the hay can be pulled back to reveal beautiful clean potatoes, there for the picking, without so much as putting a spade in the ground. This display makes use of other cunning organic wheezes, such as using squares of carpet underlay around the brassicas, preventing the cabbage root fly from laying eggs there.

To show us that organic gardening is versatile, we can now visit a rose garden, just as beautiful as those you may have seen before, but one on which no chemical fungicides or insecticides ever need to be sprayed. The trick is to choose resistant varieties and to attract predators that live on the pests that can damage roses. In the case of greenfly, plants can be grown which attract the aphid-guzzling hoverfly. And if blue tits can be encouraged to stay throughout the winter, they will feed on the overwintering eggs. Don't forget to suspend fat from canes driven into the soil near rose bushes during the winter and the birds will be grateful, the greenfly devoured.

By now you will be surprised at how much you're learning about these safe methods of husbandry, and learning in the most interesting and enjoyable way. The next garden demonstrates how all these various points can be combined to make the sort of garden you might like to have at home. There are borders of flowers, vegetables and ornamental plants, a vegetable plot which enables, by use of raised beds and paths, gardening in all weathers without risk of compacting the soil. There's a small pond to attract frogs, your own personal slug control squad, and climbing plants on the fence to give nesting sites for birds.

Having seen a 'tame' garden, the tour leads us on to a wildlife garden. Now, we might be forgiven for imagining that you'd need a fair acreage to indulge in a wildlife garden – but this is not necessarily so, as we can see here. A wildflower meadow is but a circle in an ordinary lawn. The birds are attracted to nest here by being provided with green shelves on the fence, over which a climber grows to provide shelter. The choice of planting attracts butterflies, bees, newts, birds, voles, frogs – a huge range of wildlife. What an excellent idea to give your garden, or part of your garden, over to this sort of man-made habitat. Children will love it – and love you for it.

Trees are an important feature of the landscape, enhancing any vista, and although most of us haven't enough space for a plantation of trees, here we can enjoy the willow coppice. Willows are very fast-growing and the excess growth is usefully shredded to produce regular supplies of mulch. (Don't try to copy this idea in *your* garden, unless you can plant well-away from the house, as the roots of willows will seek out drains and can cause much damage.) Providing further shelter is another group of the most important hardwood species that used to be found in the UK. These were once used specifically by craftsmen, and their presence at Ryton is another nice example of the informative nature of the gardens.

Now it's time to work back into the central area again to see the *All Muck and Magic* TV garden. Tiny as it is, it's teeming with all the ideas of mixed planting, wildlife attraction and the greedy use of every inch of space. Best of all, it's clear for all to see that a garden like this is not too difficult to create or to maintain. I think this must be one of the most popular spots in the whole of Ryton and visitors are often to be seen dallying here, taking notes and photographs, probably with the intention of copying some or all of the ideas packed into this little garden.

I said earlier that gardening takes one into other realms of interest and as we've already seen we can be involved in wildlife, the sciences and even a little history, through realizing that it's only since the introduction of chemical fertilizers and insecticides in comparatively recent years that we have to consciously garden as our ancestors used to – organically. We've seen a little domestic history, too, in the hardwood trees grown in the past for craftsmen to use. And now, but fear not, we have a little politics!

There is a list of seeds drawn up by the European Community and the government, and it is now an offence to sell seeds other than those on this UK National List or EC Common Catalogue.

Sadly, many varieties failed to be elected to this list and very often these varieties have qualities that are much more desirable to the home-grower than are the permitted ones, which invariably are chosen with commercial interests to the fore. So the HDRA have established a Seed Library, with a display garden to go with it. Members are able to 'borrow' these 'illegal' seeds from the library, grow them for their own use and become Seed Guardians of a particular variety, producing seed which is then distributed free to other members. Without the Ryton Seed Library many interesting and flavoursome fruit and vegetable varieties would disappear altogether. Joining the HDRA can turn you into a true conservationist.

The next area we pass through shows us methods of land clearance and weed control. The heavy work of digging over or rotovating tracts of weed-infested land can be eliminated by using light-excluding mulches, like the ones I've described earlier. This does mean that the ground is out of production for a whole year, but what an energy saver, and at a pinch you could plant potatoes through slits in the mulch material. At the end of the year most weeds will have given up the ghost. This area shows other methods of weed control and then passes us nicely on to wonder at the collection of unusual vegetables, most of them attractive enough to be given a prominent position in your flower border, or even grown up a trellis to decorate the house walls.

Every bit of garden space is used in a good organic garden; crops are planted in closer proximity and can still give excellent results because their roots are living the life of Riley (whoever that was) in nutritious, richly fertile soil. The elements are something over which we have less control, but here the presence of a polythene tunnel shows us that crops can be produced all the year round. It might be a good idea for me to enclose the bottom half of my garden in a huge bubble of polythene; it just might stop me moaning about the cold, the wet and the short season in my northern garden.

A great deal of interest is kindled whenever the words 'pest control' are uttered and the HDRA have many weird and wonderful ways of coping with all sorts of pest problems. The display at Ryton shows lots of the techniques which can be employed, from companion planting to an intriguing arrangement of marshalling small armies of beetles into a confined area to control slugs. For the greenhouse owner there are examples of control over whitefly and red spider mite using imported parasites and predators. Disease-resistant varieties for the greenhouse are displayed here too – something for everybody.

Lawns are not forgotten either, and the demonstration lawn shows that organic lawn care works well. There are suggestions and helpful hints on every aspect of gardening and all methods are explained clearly to the visitor.

The next port of call on our garden tour is always a high spot for me. I could have said that it always gives me a buzz, but when I tell you that it's the bee garden, I think you'll know why I declined! During the summer there is an observation bee-hive and it's fascinating to watch the incessant ativities and search out the queen bee among the workers. The garden surrounding it is planted with specially chosen flowers which, because of their pollen and nectar, are particularly attractive to bees. The fact that they are also invariably attractive to us is a further delight.

One of the interesting aspects of being a member of the HDRA is that you're invited to take part in experiments, and a plot at Ryton is set aside to show what is being done in areas of investigation such as pest and disease control, or checking out a new seed variety.

Soft fruits and top fruits are given a great deal of attention. Various forms of training the bushes and trees are displayed and ideas for windshields and a choice of varieties are there for your scrutiny. There's an apiary, too, where four colonies of bees are kept and these do the job of pollinating all the crops in the gardens. Lucky bees to have free access to such harmless and prolific flowers.

HRH Prince Charles is our patron, and a very involved and concerned patron at that, and there are wildflowers at Ryton growing from seed collected on his estate at Highgrove House. These and other insect-attracting plants are grown in small beds among the fruit section because they will bring in the predatory insects which in turn will feed on the fruit tree pests. Other mehods of control are codling moth traps and plum fruit moth traps.

A garden has been constructed at Ryton for people with special needs, which is also used for teacher training, and serves as a memorial garden for the HDRA's founder and his wife, Lawrence and Cherry Hills. The whole project is in fact a wonderfully apt way of commemorating the life and work of this remarkable couple.

Your tour is now complete and it's time to call in at the café where the food is not only delicious but as wholesome, organic and beneficial as the plants you've been admiring in the garden. There are two banks of alpines close by, there are seats outside and organic wine to sip and appreciate. What a lovely end to your day out at Ryton. The *Good Food Guide* has recommended it and all profits go towards the HDRA's research programme.

You haven't had any shopping time yet. Do wander around the shop. There are seeds, tools, books, cards, gifts, food, cosmetics, wine, jewellery, china – need I continue? Once more, all the profits go towards scientific research into improving environmentally-safe growing techniques at the gardens here.

The HDRA is an entirely independent charity and relies totally on support from members and friends. I am sure you will be impressed with the thinking behind the organic movement and certainly with the results. I can only urge you to join the ever-growing band of people who care so much for this beautiful natural world of ours and who feel that they want to take on the responsibility of improving their own little corner of it.

There's more to it than that, though. The sense of satisfaction in knowing that you are doing as much as is humanly possible to counteract the destruction of our environment and wildlife is a good feeling. Finally, belonging to the HDRA brings you in touch with so many charming, caring and kind, like-minded people. Do you wonder it's one of my favourite places to visit?

If you would like to find out more about the work of the HDRA as well as how to join the association, write to the HDRA at Ryton Gardens, Ryton-on-Dunsmore, Coventry CV8 3LG (or telephone (0203) 303517).

Afterword

I believe it to be a wholly instinctive need in all of us to be creative – a need not always recognised or fostered, but if given scope to develop one which can bring greater harmony into our lives. Painting, writing, the performing arts, the bearing and raising of children are all easily recognisable as creative pursuits but rarely, I think, do people consider the growing of plants as such. After all we are surrounded by them. They are just 'there', aren't they? And not only in gardens. Trees are growing in streets – for goodness sake. Somehow their roots are finding nourishment under all that stone, concrete or tarmac; they are still managing to flourish in that ghastly, heavily polluted air and completing their seasonal cycle. Amazing!

Look upwards in almost any city street and you will see plants of all kinds sprouting out of guttering, chimney stacks and loose brickwork – their seeds having been dropped by birds or blown by the wind into an hospitable morsel of 'gunge' – probably not soil as we know it, just an amalgam of wind-blown vegetation.

How do they do it? Yes folks, its all part of the same inherent need to create, to survive. That's what makes gardening so easy, so rewarding:

everything you try to grow wants to grow. That is its lifetime ambition, its raison d'être – it is totally on your side. Every reason then to give it the best possible environment in which to grow well and bring the greatest joy to you, the gardener.

I think you will be able to judge from the photographs in the book that from an unpromising start my garden has flourished. It is healthy and productive, its been a labour of love. The pleasure and peace it brings far outweighs the failures and battles with the elements. It is a haven for wildlife, because it is safe. The transformation hasn't cost a fortune but in the last two years it has had to change quite radically for three reasons. Firstly, since I changed the pattern of my working life I can no longer give as much of my time to the garden. Secondly, Jo who helped me so admirably for so many years had to move away to another area. She loves my garden almost as much as I do and although she can no longer give me regular help as in the past, she comes to join me in a 'blitz' whenever things get out of hand. As her move coincided with a back injury she now lectures in organic gardening to some very lucky students! The third reason, and one which we must all face eventually, is that one day advancing years will mean that much of the hard work must be reduced. I have always known that my garden was labour intensive so I have started to take steps to cut down in the workload.

My new gardener, Geoff, is much happier than I ever was to cut grass so the narrow winding path which ran the length of the garden has been widened considerably to become an irregularly shaped lawn. The unexpected effect of this has been to make the garden seem very much larger and this change has come along now my two grandsons need more space for their energetic games when they visit, so we are all happy. The extension of the path was for one reason and another delayed until the first week in December, not the best time of year to lay new turf. It happened to be a very wet winter but not a frosty one and by some miracle it survived. We had taken the opportunity once the old turf was lifted to rid the ground of as many perennial weeds as possible and to add a good amount of sand to the surface area to give better drainage.

As to the rockery, well there are already several low-growing shrubs to which I am adding several more interspersed with bulbs intended to flow through the seasons. These hopefully should cut down the need to weed and constantly remove moss, which used to become interwoven with spreading rockery plants. Widening the grassy area has also cut out a sizeable amount of the cultivated ground. Many of the original plants have found new homes in other peoples gardens and some have been relocated in mine. Some of the growing areas have been flagged over and I now limit my vegetables to those that can manage on their own without too much attention, the most successful being members of the onion and bean families. The timed drip-feed hose takes care of drought problems and fleece over salad has proved wonderfully protective. All things change and this is certainly the case in my garden.

Yes, thankfully, all things change and this is so very true of today's attitude to the problems of the environment and to the organic movement. I am overjoyed to see how the public have become deeply concerned about commercial pressures in food production.

This enlightenment has taken place gradually over the past few years but is now in such high profile that even the great multi-national firms engaged in experiments, and worse than that in on-going production of genetically modified crops, have had to accept disruption caused by public opinion. How many of us really understand the anti-oxidants, E numbers, emulsifiers, preservatives etc. in those long lists of ingredients in ready-prepared foodstuffs – and most importantly, what collective effects they may have on our health? How many of the foods we buy don't even give information about their source, growing conditions and additives? Certainly not fruit, vegetables and wine, not even the flour in our daily bread. So how do we protect ourselves from all these uncertainties? Buy organic food? Yes, but it is often far too expensive for many people to afford, and yet if we compare it to the inflated prices of processed food I think you will find it surprisingly favourable.

Added to this, of course, is the comforting thought that you are feeding yourself and your family on wholesome food produced with integrity and tasting – oh – so much better than anything else you could buy.

Best of all though, if you can, do grow your own fresh produce. No garden? think about an allotment: very cheap to rent – wonderful exercise – and there are always 'old hands' there, only to willing to give advice to new gardeners. My final farewell is to wish you may take a new interest in 'gardening the natural way' thereby gaining great happiness and good health with a clear conscience.

Reward

I've worked in the garden
Since dawn – it's now dusk –
And there's dozens of things left to do.
I've been digging and hoeing
And sieving and sowing,
And staking delphiniums blue.

But I've watered the garden now,
Cleaned up the tools,
My nails are all torn – my back's chronic.
The remedy's simply
A lemon, a dimply
Glass and a large gin and tonic . . .
With ice of course!

Further Reading

These are some of the well-thumbed books on organic gardening which have taught and inspired, helped and reassured me over the years, or which I've consulted in the research for this book.

The Concise Herbal Encyclopedia   Donald Law
The Language of the Garden   Anne Scott James
Companion Planting   Gertrude Franck
Carrots Love Tomatoes   Louise Riotte
Vegetables Naturally   Jim Hay
Natural Pest and Disease Control   Jim Hay
How To Enjoy Your Weeds   Audrey Wynne Hatfield
Nettles – Healers of the Wild   Claire Swan
About Dandelions   Eric F.W. Powell, PhD, N.D
Cooking With Flowers   Zack Hanle
Esther Dean's Gardening Book   Esther Dean
Enchanted Garden   Tom Cuthbertson
Month By Month Organic Gardening   Lawrence Hills

The HDRA also publish a number of invaluable guides and books covering every aspect of organic gardening. Rather than singling out individual titles, let me urge you to write to the HDRA for a list and discover them for yourself.

HDRA
Ryton Gardens
Ryton-on-Dunsmore
Coventry CV8 3LG
Tel: (0203) 303517